The Power of Positive Selling

30 Surefire Techniques to Win
New Clients, Boost Your Commission,
and Build the Mindset for Success

Stephan Schiffman

NEW YORK   CHICAGO   SAN FRANCISCO
LISBON   LONDON   MADRID   MEXICO CITY   MILAN
NEW DELHI   SAN JUAN   SEOUL   SINGAPORE
SYDNEY   TORONTO

1 2 3 4 5 6 7 8 9 10   DOC/DOC   1 6 5 4 3 2 1

ISBN: 978-0-07-178870-0
MHID: 0-07-178870-0

e-ISBN: 978-0-07-178871-7
e-MHID: 0-07-178871-9

Interior design by Mauna Eichner and Lee Fukui.

McGraw-Hill books are available at special quantity discounts to use as premiums and sales promotions or for use in corporate training programs. To contact a representative, please e-mail us at bulksales@mcgraw-hill.com.

This book is printed on acid-free paper.

To Justin Eli

CONTENTS

PART III   FROM START TO CLOSE

ACKNOWLEDGMENTS

My sincere thanks for the success of this project go to Monika Verma, Gary Krebs, Donya Dickerson, Tom Jared, Darren Newton, Anthony Bartolo, Tobias W. Heffernan, Joshua Michael Sanders, and, of course, Anne, Daniele, and Jennifer.

Equally significant are all those salespeople who go out each day to prospect, meet new people, and make sales. These are my true inspiration. Thank you, all.

INTRODUCTION

It had been raining since nine o'clock.

The road in front of me stretched out, a bleak gray lined with the skeletons of trees that had been shorn of their leaves and were shivering in the early autumn chill. The car held a dusty, dry smell; redolent of half-eaten sandwiches and too many cups of coffee gulped down hastily in the early morning air. The windshield wipers slapped across the glass, and I could almost beat out a rhythm against the steering wheel with their *chock! chock! chock!* as I squinted through the mist, trying to make out the exit sign.

I'd been up too late the evening before, and I wasn't looking forward to the sales call I was about to make. My mouth was dry, and I felt a small, persistent headache nagging at the back of my neck. I shifted irritably in the seat and wiped a hand across my clammy forehead. My warm bed and the last cup of steaming coffee seemed hours in the past.

Several turns and one missed street later, I was staring at the front of a dull industrial building. A small plaque next to the door informed me that I'd arrived at my destination, four minutes before my 9:30 appointment. My legs ached, and I felt tired deep in my bones. I couldn't think of anywhere I'd rather be less than where I was: at the front door of another client to be wooed, charmed, placated, and ultimately added to my address book.

Another day.

Another sales call.

*   *   *   *   *

Does that sound like you? Probably at some point in your career you've had an experience similar to that. Perhaps it turned out badly—the client was grouchy, the admin who booked your appointment proved to be incompetent, and in the end you walked away with nothing but a vow to never, ever do business in that area again. Or maybe things turned around. The sun came out, the client was smiling and helpful, and you wound up at a long lunch over a couple of beers and the beginning of a fruitful relationship.

You may well have formed the idea that whichever outcome you get is more or less in the lap of fortune. But I'm here to tell you that isn't true. In the more than three decades I've been selling, I've been confronted with just about every situation you can imagine.

I've met clients who were obstinate.

Clients who were whiney.

Clients who were furious—even before I'd pitched to them.

Clients who were forgetful and who forgot I'd scheduled an appointment with them.

Clients who were pleasant right up to the moment when they had to make a decision.

I've even had—in one memorable case—a client who informed me that he couldn't discuss anything because his pet ferret had just died. I'm not kidding. Really.

And yet, amid all of this craziness, I've found ways to keep selling. There's not really a magic secret to this. I'm not supernaturally blessed with tolerance—in fact, quite the contrary. The solution is what I've come to call the Power of Positive Selling.

The concept isn't new. Norman Vincent Peale wrote a bestselling book titled *The Power of Positive Thinking*. And that was back in 1952. The book reached millions of people with a message that blended religion and psychiatry.

I don't claim to do any of that. But what I will say to you is that in my experience—my very *long* experience—the success of selling depends on three things:

1. You must believe in what you're selling.

2. You must help the client solve a problem.

3. You must approach every situation in a positive frame of mind.

If you follow these and some other rules I'm going to set out in this book, you'll find that it will have a marked effect on your sales. Your commission will go up, you'll add more names to your client and prospect lists, and you'll find it easier to close deals. Above all, you'll find yourself with a better attitude toward your job and toward life in general.

Positive selling isn't just a matter of learning some new techniques; it's a philosophy. It infects everything you do and every aspect of your life. It's not mindless, either. I'm not asking you to plod forth in the face of certain disaster, a bland smile on your face. You need to be realistic about what you're doing and assess your chances of success.

However, I don't believe you'll get anywhere if you start every sales call with failure in the forefront of your mind. You need to develop what I call "positive realism." That is, you need to look at every setback as a challenge and every challenge as an opportunity. When a client says "no," you have to ask "why?" When a client says, "Let me think about it," you have to know how to keep the conversation moving forward and not let it die an agonizing death. Above all, you've got to know how to find out what the client wants and how you can help in that quest. That's really where the sales rubber hits the road.

One thing about sales as a profession is that it's never dull. You must be prepared for the unexpected. Several years ago, I'd called on a prospect I'd known for several years. He was a very conservative fellow—he never did anything unexpected or said anything out of the ordinary. We were chatting about this and that when his admin walked into the room. He turned around to me and said, "Steve, Marla (the admin) and I are getting married next week, and I'd like you to be the best man."

My mouth practically hit the carpet. I was amazed, flattered, and overwhelmed. I started fumbling around with an answer and got something semi-coherent out. Only when I got out the door and was in my car, putting the key in the ignition, did it occur to me that the date he'd named was the date of a major sales conference at which I was scheduled to give a presentation.

My stomach hit the floor, and I felt sweat pouring over my hands. I'd committed to two conflicting events. What was I going to do?

I thought non-stop about it for the next hour as I was driving to my office. By the time I'd reached the parking lot, I had a plan. I asked a colleague to deliver the address I'd written to the sales conference. And when I stood with my friend in the front of the church as his bride walked down the aisle, I can honestly say I wasn't thinking of anything except their happiness.

Positive thinking. Positive attitude. That's what it's all about. Because anything else will make you, and everyone around you, miserable. But a positive attitude won't just get you the sale; it'll make your life happier.

PART I
PUTTING YOUR BEST FOOT FORWARD

THE REALITY
OF SELLING

t's the most basic thing trainers tell their pupils: Sales is a
numbers game.

Well, maybe. But I don't think it's a matter of reducing it to
that. Many people do, though. They have very specific metrics by
which they're going to measure your performance.

What these trainers are trying to do is quantify what you do
every day:

- What's your call-to-prospect ratio?

- How many of your prospects are you converting to leads?

- What proportion of your sales pitches are you closing?

- How's that affecting the size of your commission?

- What dollar figures are you bringing into your company?

If these numbers are generally going up, trainers assume you
must be doing something right.

I don't want to entirely discount the conventional wisdom.
After all, good numbers in all the above categories are a good
indication that you must be doing something right. They're part
of the measure of a successful, positive salesperson.

Above all, I want this book to approach the question of your attitude, which is a more abstract, complex issue.

Before we start on that, though, we've got to get some things out of the way. These have to do with the reality of selling.

In fact, there are only five things you can do to increase your income from sales:

1. **You can increase the number of dials you make.** That is to say, you can increase the number of calls, which will, in turn, proportionally increase the number of people you reach and thus improve your chances of creating a lead and closing a sale.

2. **You can improve your ratio of calls made to calls completed.** This may rest on your ability to leave compelling voice messages. It also may be contingent on your ability to bypass gatekeepers.

3. **You can schedule more appointments.** Again, this involves knowing how to deal with gatekeepers, but it also means finding ways to keep the attention of prospects and get them talking to you.

4. **You can close more sales.** This is a big one. It requires that you have a compelling story to tell your clients and for you to know what they need and how you can help them solve their problems.

5. **You can get more money per sale.** Obviously this is a broad intention with everything you do, but here there is a very concrete set of steps you'll have to take if you're going to make each sale more profitable to your company. You need to know how to motivate and close price increases and per-unit savings.

These five things are the only way you're going to improve your commission. And notice that three of the five have to do with improving your ratios. In point of fact, your ratios are one of the most important things you must keep track of during the sales cycle:

- How many calls are you making to obtain each prospect?

- How many prospects are you converting into leads?

- How many leads are offering appointments?

- How many of these appointments are ending in closed sales?

The more you track these numbers, the more aware of them you'll become and, consequently, the better you'll be at meeting your expectations.

The more in control you are of your ratios, the more you control the results. If you know that to get five prospects you need to make twenty-five sales cold calls, that gives you a clear idea of how many calls you'll have to make in order to get twenty prospects. If you're converting ten of those prospects into leads/clients, then you know what to expect in terms of how many calls you'll need to make to generate twenty clients. And if you can close with five of these clients, you've created a metric of how many calls = prospects = leads = sales.

The results may, it's true, be discouraging, but it's always better to work from specific numbers than hopeful guesses.

The formula I recommend is $A > P > s$

"A" stands for appointments; "P" stands for prospects; "S" stands for sales. Notice that the numbers (and the size of the letters) get smaller the further we go in the sequence. You'll have to make more appointments to get fewer prospects and fewer prospects to get fewer sales. But at least with some numbers you know where you are.

We might put another symbol in front of the A: CC to stand for cold calling. I'm going to tell you a secret about cold calling:

I don't like to do it. In point of fact, almost no one in Sales does. But the best salespeople have worked out an understanding of where cold calling fits into the process of creating closed sales, and for that reason they've learned to do it—and do it well.

What it comes down to is this: To do cold calling, you need to pick up the phone and dial a number. A given number of cold calls will create a series of appointments (calls-to-appointments is another ratio you must keep careful track of). The appointments mean the possibility of prospects, which, in turn, gives you the opportunity to close sales.

The biggest mistake that salespeople make is to stop in this sequence somewhere short of the final step. They say, "Well, Steve, the most important thing our sales force does is to generate appointments."

My reply is always, "Appointments are good. You can't get anywhere without talking to the client in person. But how many of those appointments end in actual closed sales." At which point the conversation gets very quiet.

The point is *not* to stop during the sequence. That's a recipe for disaster, because the whole point of sales is to keep the conversation with the client moving forward. If you say to yourself, "Well, I've established rapport with the client" or "At least he and I can talk now," you're giving up too early. Chances are that your conversation is never going to go much beyond the preliminaries.

Instead, keep your eyes on the prize: that magic moment when you say to the client, "Well, I think we've got a deal." If you're not getting to that point, you're not really selling. You're just doing all the steps up to the moment when a sale becomes final. Let's go back and examine those five steps we can take to improve our sales numbers.

1. **Increase the number of calls.** This doesn't sound too hard. If you're making twenty-five calls a day, why not make thirty? Heck, why not make thirty-five. But

here's where positive selling comes in: If the only reason you're making these calls is to somehow improve your numbers in this ratio, you're missing the point. You want to increase the number of calls you make because you genuinely believe that you can find more prospects among them. If you make these calls with a strong, positive attitude, you'll find that your rewards will be all out of proportion to the increased number of calls you make.

2. **Get through to more people.** The biggest obstacle these days to this objective is the presence of gatekeepers: all those whose job it is to prevent you from talking to their boss. Any salesperson recognizes this: The administrative assistants, senior aides, and senior secretaries can be problematic. Again, a positive approach is one of your biggest assets here. Too many salespeople are defeated early on because they don't want to take the time and trouble to woo or circumnavigate gatekeepers. Salespeople also need to learn the art of leaving compelling messages on voicemail. Most voicemails aren't returned. But you need to make sure yours are.

3. **Schedule more appointments.** A commandment of the positive salesperson is this: Be specific. You won't get anywhere in sales if you don't learn to nail things down. The more precise you are about what you want and when and how you want it, the more people will respond with specific commitments. So when you talk to a prospect, always get an agreement to talk again at a particular time and place: "Mr. X, I think we've had a very good discussion today and I'd like to continue it. What do you say we meet next Tuesday at 3 PM. I'll speak to your admin on the way out and set it up." Here you've taken the initiative to propose something and to make sure it's on Mr. X's calendar.

4. **Close sales.** Closing sales is an art. I've even devoted several books to it. It's not something that you can learn lightly. But like anything else in sales, closing is in part a matter of attitude as well as technique. The trick to closing is to present the client with the necessity of committing. It's not enough for him to think abstractly that he should buy what you're selling. He needs to make a firm commitment to your proposal of a solution to his problem. If he can't do that, then you've not made a strong enough case to him—and you need to go back and do it.

Selling, as I've said to salespeople for years, is not a matter of learning a special technique or a particular set of responses to challenges. It's a philosophy. An attitude. It's a belief that what you're offering the client is important.

If you start from the point of view that the client's interests and yours coincide, you can find a way to make a win-win situation for both of you. This is the Holy Grail of sales; it's what you strive for. And you'll find, as I'll remind you all the way throughout this book, that the key is your attitude: the importance of positive selling.

WHO BUYS AND WHO DOESN'T

2

Truestory.

A couple of years ago I pitched my sales development program to a new company. I wasn't too sure about what reception I'd get—the company was one I'd never dealt with before, and I didn't know too much about it except that it seemed to be an up-and-comer in its chosen field of commerce. I knew, from long experience, that new companies often have a sense of arrogance about their operations, a conviction that the old guys (like me) have done it wrong for a lot of years and it's their job to set us old geezers right. Because of my sense of this attitude, I didn't want to start things off on the wrong foot.

I began my presentation, therefore, in a way I usually don't. I set down my notes, turned off the PowerPoint presentation, and said, "All right. Why don't you guys tell me how to sell?"

There was a moment of completely blank silence. You'd think I'd asked them to solve Fermat's Theorem. I could see the confused stares between the executives who'd invited me in, and I could almost hear the comments:

"We invited this guy? And now he's asking us to teach him?"

There was a method in my madness, though. I knew that if I simply laid out my commandments of selling, the result of decades in the business, the reaction would be one of disdain.

After all, it was a brave new world out there. What could I possibly know about a world dominated by social media, Twitter, and an ever-changing technical landscape? But if I made it clear that I was willing to learn, that I wanted them to teach me, I stood a much better chance of being taken seriously.

Sure enough, after a moment the comments began to flow:

- Stay in touch with the customer.

- Listen to what the customer wants.

- Start a Facebook page.

- Create a company blog.

- Groupsource your customer service.

I listened, taking extensive notes, for about ten minutes. Then I raised my hand for quiet.

"How many of you," I asked, "realize that as far as I'm concerned, you're my customers?" There was another long silence. I watched them as the idea sank in.

"I'm selling salesperson training," I told them. "That's what I've been doing for a lot of years. And you guys are my customers. I need to convince you that what I'm selling is worth it. So how can I possibly do that if I don't know what you think are the most important aspects of selling?"

I could see heads nodding as this sank in. Then I followed it up.

"Selling," I said, "is about solving someone's problem. Sometimes the person you're selling to doesn't know he's got a problem, and sometimes the problem's so big that he doesn't think there's a solution. So the first thing you've got to do is *identify the problem*. Then you've got to show him what you can do about it, and finally, you've got to convince him that solving the problem is worth the price you're asking."

These comments redirected the discussion. A few minutes later, rather than coming up with a laundry list of things salespeople should do or pay attention to, the group was involved in a deep argument about the basics of selling. Above all, they were grappling with two related issues:

- Why do people buy?

- Who buys and who doesn't?

I think that these questions are at the heart of the sales process, and if you can't answer them, you need to sit down and think— and, I might add, read the rest of this book—until you can.

THE REASONS FOR BUYING

In the previous chapter, I addressed the issue of why people buy. Now we need to look at the problem of determining who buys. To some extent, the answer depends on the kind of organization you're selling to. But there's also a matter of psychology involved.

A friend of mine told me about an experience she had selling to an executive of a large company. The conversation, she says, went something like this:

Salesperson: I think you can see from what I've outlined that my service will address the problems you've been having with your servers. From what you've said, the key issue for you is efficiency and speed in your processes, is that right?

Executive: Yes. We can't afford the kind of slowness we've been experiencing.

Salesperson: Absolutely. I understand. As I've indicated, our system can guarantee an increase in speed of up to 20 percent—and it's possible that it could go higher, depending on the demands you place on the system.

Executive: That's very impressive, if you can back it up.

Salesperson: We can certainly do that. So let's talk about a timeline for installation.

Executive: Wait a minute. Before we go any further, this is going to have to be approved by the board.

Salesperson: But aren't you empowered to make those decisions? I don't want to lose any time on this, and I'm sure you don't either.

Executive: With an expenditure of this magnitude, the board has to be consulted. Also, I need to look at the disruptions to our service while the new system is being installed.

Salesperson: It seems to me that you could give me a turnaround answer in just a day or two, especially since your current system is really costing you money.

Executive: I'm sorry. I can't confirm this purchase right now. You're going to have to be patient.

Clearly, the executive saw the benefits of what my friend was selling. The problem was, he wasn't the one who was buying—it was, effectively, the board. You might say, as my friend did, that such a system is inefficient and will make it impossible for the company to make good, timely decisions. That doesn't matter. The executive wasn't going to put his job at risk to violate company procedures. My friend should have recognized this immediately and worked to establish a timeline for the sale based on the time needed to consult the board and obtain its agreement. She should have readjusted to the fact that although she was presenting to the executive, effectively her customer was the board. By pushing the executive, she raised his hackles and imperiled the sale. (Although, just to finish out the story, the sale did go through a couple of weeks later.)

IDENTIFYING THE BUYER

One of the first things any salesperson needs to do is establish this: Is the person you're talking to someone who has the authority to make the purchase? Most of the time, if you've done your homework properly, the answer will be yes. That's because by the time you're on the sales call, especially if it's one to a company you've not dealt with before, you should have a very clear picture of how the company is organized, who's who in the hierarchy, and whom you should be talking to. That avoids wasting everyone's time and makes for the most efficient call.

Sometimes, though, that's not possible. The company's organization chart may be opaque to the point where it's impossible to understand who has authority to do what. Most of the time, when this is the case, you're looking at a company in which decision making has been concentrated at the top of the pyramid. In these circumstances, when the executive you speak with says, "I have to talk to someone else to get this authorized," I counsel patience. You can get angry, of course, but it won't make a difference in the speed of the decision, and it may blow the sale.

Sometimes, it's possible to find a way around this. Imagine, for instance, the following exchange:

Salesperson: I think we've discussed the ways in which our company's widget can help your production problems and provide benefits to your company. What size order do you feel you'll need?

Executive: Just a minute. Before we say anything about the size of the order, I'm going to have to check with my boss about whether she's okay with this.

Salesperson: So your boss has the authority to okay this purchase?

Executive: Yes. It'll have to get her approval.

Salesperson: I completely understand. That's not a problem. But I wonder if it would be helpful if I were to speak to her, so I can answer any questions she may have about the widget and the benefits it provides. Could we set up a meeting next Tuesday with the three of us to discuss this?

Executive: That's possible, I guess. I'll check and see if her schedule's open and get back to you tomorrow.

Salesperson: I appreciate it. I'll give you a call tomorrow just to check where we stand. How's ten o'clock work for you?

In this conversation, the salesperson accepts the limitations of the company's concentrated lines of authority. Rather than argue or try to get the executive to do an end run around his boss—both of which could have disastrous consequences—she lays the groundwork for another conversation, this one with the person authorized to okay the sale. Notice that she doesn't leave it to the executive to take the initiative on this. She sets up a specific time the following day for them to talk. This is positive selling at its best: using what at first glance appears to be a setback to gain a further step in knowing more about the company, its officers, and its structure. If the salesperson can forge a relationship with the executive's boss, she's that much further along in creating a long-term sales relationship with the company.

Encountering Psychological Resistance

In my book *The 25 Toughest Sales Objections,* I talk about the challenges of selling to someone who avoids decisions. Some elements of this are present in the passive-aggressive personality, a topic I'll talk about later in this book. But for right now I want to discuss briefly how to deal with someone who just hates making a decision. Unlike the cases above, where the client wasn't authorized to buy, this is an instance where the client has the authorization but doesn't want to use it.

I don't, in general, have an easy time dealing with indecisive people. Part of me always wants to lean across the table, grab them by the collar, and yell, "What I'm asking you to do isn't that complicated! It's not rocket science! Just decide!"

Fortunately, in a career spanning a large number of years, I've never done that. Instead, I've had to learn to swallow my anger and focus on why the client doesn't want to decide to buy.

I think this comes down to the following reasons:

1. The client has, in the past, made a decision that had adverse consequences and therefore is frightened of repeating the error.

2. The client doesn't like what you're selling but wants to avoid a confrontation with you by putting off a decision.

3. The client has some hidden reason for avoiding a decision—for instance, waiting for an offer from one of your rivals.

There may be more reasons, but these are the major ones I think you'll run into.

The only way to find out which of these issues is at the root of the problem is to keep asking questions. This is difficult, because the client is, consciously or unconsciously, hiding from you the reason for his decision, and he may resent your probing. But I encourage you to keep it up as long as possible, precisely because you have to know what you're dealing with.

In regard to number three, if you establish that the client is playing you off against a competitor, you'll have to decide if you want to improve on your offer. Or, if you don't believe that benefits you sufficiently, you can walk away from the deal—a drastic decision but sometimes warranted.

Concerning number two, you've got to convince the client that saying no to you won't imperil your relationship. This is essential, because you're trying to lay the foundation of a long-term sales relationship, and it can't be broken by one failed sale.

And in regard to number one? This is one of the hardest ones because you're dealing with a complicated psychological problem. Some people have been so intimidated by a bad decision that they want to avoid ever making another one. What they really want in this case is iron-clad assurance that this sale is going to turn out all right.

I recommend with such people that you set up a systematic, detailed schedule for follow up. Make it clear to them that if something goes wrong, you'll be at their side, explaining matters to their boss, fixing the problem, and making sure that it never, ever happens again. It's possible that you'll still run into resistance, but a positive approach like this is likely to take you a very long way toward overcoming that psychological block and winning the sale.

WHY PEOPLE BUY FROM YOU

3

A good friend of mine who's a professor at a college in New York invited me to come to one of his classes. I arrived a bit early and we sat in his office, sipping coffee and talking. Finally, it was time to go to class.

We went down the hallway and into a large lecture hall. There must have been 200 or so students, lounging in their chairs, some of them busily texting on their phones, others chattering to one another, some propped against one another quietly snoring. A few of them even looked as though they were studying. I dropped into a seat at the back of the hall, while the professor made his way to the lectern.

I expected once he got there that he'd have to blow a whistle or an air horn or something to get everyone's attention. The volume of noise in the room hadn't sensibly diminished when we entered, and I wondered if this was typical of the way these classes worked.

The professor stood behind the lectern and pulled some notes out of his briefcase. He paused, straightened his glasses, and looked out at the audience. Then a funny thing happened: They all shut up. Instantly. And completely. You could have heard a pin drop as he began to speak.

I gave a good deal of thought over the next hour of the class as to how he'd accomplished this miracle, gaining everyone's undivided attention and holding it in an iron grip. When class was over and we were walking back to his office, I asked how he did it.

He shrugged. "I think they just know it's important to listen to me. They want to pass the class, and they know I've got what they need to pass it. So they're motivated to be quiet and listen."

It made sense, but I couldn't help wondering if there was more to it than that. I've seen speakers, after all, who couldn't hold an audience in place if you gave them fifty sets of handcuffs. I've watched salespeople who struggle to put their point across and keep the meeting on track. So the ease with which my friend accomplished this was something to admire and, if possible, emulate.

A POSITIVE PRESENCE

I put some of it down to that ineffable quality called "presence." I can't precisely define presence, but as a Supreme Court justice once said about pornography, I know it when I see it. Presence is that sense that a speaker radiates absolute control, combined with knowledge of her or his subject, married to a charismatic personality. Great political speakers are masters of presence.

Winston Churchill, one of the most admired speakers of the twentieth century, believed in detailed preparation for his speeches in the House of Commons. He would carefully rehearse his remarks, memorizing them and going over them obsessively. The result, of course, was that he marshaled the English language in defense of Great Britain against Nazi Germany and rallied the people behind him as no one had done since the days of Henry V at Agincourt.

From every account, Churchill was also a master of presence. When he rose to speak in the House, people paid attention. This was despite the fact—not known to many people nowadays— that Churchill suffered from a speech defect. His teeth were sufficiently uneven that when he pronounced the letter *s*, it was with a slight whistling sound. He struggled, as a young man, to overcome this and when he couldn't, he simply carried on, relying on the power of his words and the force of his personality to win the day.

I think we can agree that he was successful in this endeavor.

Presence is a quality I believe all salespeople should strive for. We don't all have to be Churchill. Very few people can, except for Churchill himself. But he's a good model to emulate.

Presence doesn't always have to be expressed through speech. You can have a presence that will command a room's attention by the way you hold yourself, by the way you move, and above all by your belief in yourself and what you're doing. Here are some practical suggestions in that regard:

1. **Stand and walk firmly and decisively.** Don't slouch, don't shuffle, and don't stare at the ground. Good posture is more than just an ideal physical habit. It projects a psychological confidence that will impress other people. When walking, don't rush—life's not a race. If you're walking with someone, match your stride to theirs.

2. **Look directly at the person or people you're talking to.** Not meeting their gaze will mark you out as shifty and dishonest, or at least as having something to hide. When listening to someone during a conversation, give little signals now and then, such as nodding your head, to show that you're interested in and absorbing what they're saying.

3. **Smile.** You don't have to keep a fixed grin on your face (which would probably make people think you've been

drinking or something), but don't scowl all the time. No one likes a grouch, and you shouldn't look or act like one.

4. **When greeting clients, or anyone else, give a short, firm handshake and a smile.** Trying to crush the other person's hand makes you seem like a jerk, and giving a limp fish handshake gives the impression of indecision.

5. **If you're speaking to a large group of people, pitch your voice so everyone can hear without straining.** There's no need to shout; the power of your voice comes from the diaphragm, the belt of muscle just below your stomach. Use that to push out your voice so it reaches everyone in the room. (If this sounds confusing, practice it for a while. You'll find, if you do it properly, that you can speak in a large room without straining your voice.)

BEING POSITIVE DURING A SALES CALL

I've chosen to talk about professional presence toward the beginning of this book because a lot of the rest of what I'm going to tell you flows from it. It's not the same thing at all as intimidation. The very last thing you want to do is try to intimidate or overwhelm the client. Rather, you want to radiate an atmosphere of positivity.

In other words, you want to be absolutely confident in what you're selling, and confident that the client needs it. I believe this confidence flows from your inner core, a belief in yourself and your company. During a lot of sales pitches, you'll run into unexpected obstacles, some of them surprising. You'll have to think on your feet and cope with strange requests and objections. But none of that should ever ruffle the surface of your self-confidence and positivity.

The client will buy from you because he genuinely believes what you're selling will improve his business. And you have to believe that as well. This means you have to ask questions that will show you what precisely the client wants and then figure out how what you're selling meets that need. Your questions should reflect your positive approach.

Consider, for instance, the situation in which you want to find out something about your client's perception of the changing marketplace. This is a very common issue these days, as the United States economy undergoes a series of structural transformations, the likes of which most of us haven't seen before. It's important that you understand where your client's company fits into all this. So how can you ask about it?

Here are some questions salespeople commonly use:

- What is it about this economy that's hurting you guys the most?

- Are you seeing your customer base contract?

- What are the biggest obstacles you face to your supply chain?

- Which of your competitors is the greatest threat to you right now?

These are all perfectly valid and important questions, and knowing the answers will be a big help in figuring out how to create a solution to your client's problems. But think of how much better it would be if you could ask those same questions in a slightly different way:

- What opportunities does the new economy offer you?

- As your customer base changes, where are new customers coming from?

- How can you readjust your supply chain to take advantage of new opportunities?

- What are some advantages you hold over your competition right now?

All these questions get at exactly the same issues as the first list. But because they're phrased positively, they push the client toward thinking of solutions rather than just seeing the problems.

I don't say that you shouldn't recognize problems when they exist. Right now, a lot of companies are struggling desperately to keep their heads above water, and there are big problems, not only in the United States but abroad, with economic and social stability. But if you start with how big the difficulty is, it'll be easy for you and the client to talk yourselves into a hole from which you won't emerge.

Maintaining a strong sense of confidence helps you avoid these pitfalls. You know you've got the solutions the client is looking for. It's a matter of finding them. As long as you keep that in the forefront of your mind and project that to everyone you speak to, you'll do fine.

Extend that confidence into the rest of your life as well. I believe too few salespeople do this. Every morning they get out of bed and say to themselves, whether silently or out loud, "Oh, God, here we go again!" Hold onto that attitude long enough and every part of your working day will become a burden.

In my experience, there are two kinds of salespeople: those who look on sales as a job and those who believe it's a career. The sales-as-jobs people are the ones who look and act miserable. They're the ones who are staggering out of bed every morning, wishing desperately they could crawl back under the covers. Some of them will have successful sales and make big commissions, but those successes are much more likely to go to the salespeople who understand that sales is a career. It's a long-term proposition in which you'll get the opportunity to look at virtually every aspect of your clients' companies, see the strengths and weaknesses, and work with the clients to make things better.

Of course, career salespeople also have mornings when they'd prefer to go back to bed. I have that feeling more than I care to say. Keeping focused and positive, however, is going to make those occasions fewer and farther between. And, perhaps most important, it'll make people want to buy from you.

IT'S ALL ABOUT ATTITUDE

4

Anyone who's ever lived in New York City will tell you that in New York, taxi drivers are a breed apart. I've lived here for many years, and even after all that acclimation, I still sit in the back of cabs, my hands covering my eyes, as the drivers negotiate streets at speeds that would be unsafe if they were driving the Indianapolis Speedway. Some New York taxi drivers tend to completely ignore pedestrians. In my experience, if you ask one of them about pedestrians, he'll give an answer along these lines:

1. Pedestrians are the enemy.

2. Pedestrians are food.

3. *What* pedestrians?

Nonetheless, I continue to find cab driving in New York a source of entertainment and stimulation, as well as acute terror. That's because it's one of the purest expressions I know of Attitude. Not "attitude," which is a wimpy buzzword that's used by overpaid image consultants. But Attitude. With a capital A.

The New York cab driver starts a fare with a very simple approach: He wants to get somewhere—say, from Park Avenue and 56th—to somewhere else—perhaps Times Square at 42nd and Broadway. And he wants to do it in the fastest, simplest, most direct way possible. The fact that traffic on Park Avenue is at a standstill because of a fender bender on 44th Street has absolutely no relevance for him. He could care less. He wants to get to his destination, because the sooner he makes it there, the more fares he can pick up. Thus he discounts the various obstacles in his way: traffic, stop lights, slow-moving pedestrians. Traffic lights? Suggestions, nothing more. Slow traffic blocking the street? That's what curbs are for. Pedestrians? Well, we've already dealt with that. The cab driver in New York starts out with nothing more than a goal and an Attitude.

Oh, and a passenger. Let's not forget the passenger.

ATTITUDE AS THE BASIS OF POSITIVE SELLING

Good salesmanship is a combination of a lot of things, including research, knowledge of the product or service you're selling, respect for your client, and belief in yourself and your company. But deep down, a bit of it is Attitude. Not necessarily the take-no-prisoners-damn-the-torpedoes Attitude of a New York cab driver. But a positive Attitude about what you're doing.

This isn't always the easiest thing in the world. At the beginning of this book I mentioned my experience one gray morning, heading out to a sales call in a driving rain. I've had other situations, equally dire, including being stuck in a snow storm on the Pennsylvania Turnpike for three hours, blocked by an overturned eight-wheeler. Such things can dampen your enthusiasm.

But positive selling isn't about being a pollyanna, and it's not about giving up either. It's about understanding the value of what you're doing and maintaining a strong, affirmative approach, even during the most depressing sales call. Fundamentally, I think, deep down you've got to feel good about life.

I had some opportunity to test this theory a while ago. I had flown in from New York to Chicago to speak to a group of sales managers at a conference. My flight was delayed for two hours at O'Hare Airport in Chicago. I found myself constantly bumping into groups of screaming teenagers on their way to a school retreat, and the cabbie from the airport got lost three times trying to find the building where I was headed. At that moment, I hated Chicago, teenagers, and the cab driver. The sky was gloomy, and the hotel where the conference was being held was ugly and dirty.

On top of which, it was my birthday—the last day when I wanted to be away from home, working.

By the time I got to the conference itself, I was just about ready to tell the cab driver to turn the damn cab around and go back to the airport. But I got a grip on myself. These people, I told myself, paid a lot of money for you to talk to them. And they're expecting you to be good. They deserve the best you can give them.

I walked up to the podium, shook hands with the person chairing the sessions, and spent the next two hours having more fun than I'd had in some time. The group was energetic, responsive, lively, and challenging. I could feel the energy coming from them to me in waves, invigorating me. The more I interacted with them, the better I felt. By the time I got back into a cab the next day to return to O'Hare, I was feeling wonderful about Chicago. It's a great city. I love it. The cab driver was friendly and talkative, and I gave him a big tip. At the airport I even managed to smile at a couple of teenagers who were wandering down the concourse. And the flight back to New York was calm, with no turbulence, and felt like a dream.

WHERE DOES ATTITUDE COME FROM?

One of the points of that story is that Attitude can turn a bad situation around. A second, very important point is that Attitude is more than what you bring into a sale; it's what you take from it. Actors will say that one of the hardest things to do is put on a show in front of an unresponsive audience. Having done some amateur acting in my (very) younger days, I can confirm this notion. If you're standing on stage, saying your lines, and nothing comes back from beyond the footlights, you can feel the energy drain out of you. On the other hand, if you can hear murmurs, laughter, and applause, you'll find your performance improving, perhaps even reaching heights you didn't think were possible.

So part of the point here is to learn to take what your audience is giving you. Use their questions and comments to reinforce your own enthusiasm for what you're selling.

This is yet another reason why, for me, questions are central to the sales process. By asking your client questions, you get her feedback—and you can use that feedback to better understand what she finds helpful and important about your product or service. That understanding, in turn, improves your Attitude.

I found an interesting example of this concept in a story a friend of mine told me about a sale he was making. He was selling software and had spent several weeks in a dry spell. Most of his sales had either gone south completely or had been bogged down in seemingly endless negotiation of the finer points of the contract. He felt, he told me later, as if every morning he went out and hurled himself against a brick wall. He fell back, battered and bruised, and he couldn't see that it was making any significant difference to the wall.

On this particular sales call, he was selling to a large company that already had software that covered a lot of the functions of his product. So his challenge was to find something it could do that was different—was it better, faster, more efficient? Did it have greater functionality? Was it less expensive?

He had considered all these questions and hadn't been able to come up with satisfactory answers by the morning of the call. All the way there, he found himself thinking, *Well, I'll go through the motions, she'll say no, and then I'll be back in the car, heading for lunch.* In other words, he was half defeated before he started.

He went into the conference room, shook hands with the department head whom he'd contacted, and began running through his presentation. About halfway through, he noticed that she didn't seem to be paying as much attention but was tapping notes into her BlackBerry.

Great! he thought. *Now it's* really *over. She hasn't been listening to a thing I've said.* He cleared his throat and asked, "Can you tell me about the satisfaction level with your current system?"

She studied her notes for a minute and then said, "Well, as I'm sure you know, our system that we have now performs the functions you're offering, and I don't see much reason to change."

Mentally, my friend began to gather his things together and prepare for departure. But there was a "but" in her voice that made him pause.

"But," she said, "I was looking at what you've said about compatibility issues. The biggest problem we have with our current software is that it's written for larger networks. When we use it in smaller networks, it becomes less efficient. What I like about what you're selling is that it might work for our divisions overseas, which are a lot smaller."

My friend felt his heart jump twelve feet. In a voice that, he tells me, was a bit unsteady, he said, "Could you tell me something more about the needs of the overseas divisions?"

I won't go into the rest of the call. Suffice it to say, by the time it was all over, my friend had been introduced to the vice president who was responsible for the company's overseas operations, and they had been able to find a number of places in which the software of my friend's company would be markedly superior to what the client's company was using. The sky was suddenly blue, birds were singing, and my friend told me that he ate the best lunch of his life after the sales call.

What I learned from this story is that sometimes it's the client who has the insight into what you're selling that enables you to put the deal across. After all, who knows the company better than its executives? They may well be able to show you—given the opportunity—how what you're selling can have benefits beyond those you envision. If you've got the proper Attitude, you'll pick up that football and run with it all the way to the goal line.

WALK THE LINE

I don't necessarily recommend that you adopt New York cab drivers as your Attitude models, despite the way I started this chapter. Attitude, after all, can be carried too far. Some salespeople in my experience even think it's a substitute for all the other components of positive selling. With Attitude, they feel, you can bulldoze your way over the client, ignoring his needs and concerns.

In a previous book, *25 Toughest Sales Objections (And How to Overcome Them)*, I identify four types of clients: Dominant, Influence, Steadiness, and Conscientious. In the book, I make recommendations on how to approach each of these groups. All of these groups, I suggest, can also be found among salespeople.

Dominants are one of the most common types. They're all about Attitude. They're aggressive, pushy, demanding, and assertive. They won't take anything on faith, and they tend to shove objections out of the way like—well, like a New York cab driver negotiating Fifth Avenue during rush hour.

For a salesperson, the down side of having this kind of personality is you exclude the client from the conversation. The client becomes, figuratively, the pedestrian to your cab driver. He's just another obstacle for you to overcome, and any questions or concerns he has can easily be pushed aside.

An approach like that may get sales—there are lots of clients who are intimidated by pushy, aggressive salespeople—but it won't build long-term relationships. In fact, it's much more likely to put people off and convince them never to work with you or your company. Clients want to know that you're interested in what they do. They want you to help them solve problems. That means cooperation and finding mutually beneficial solutions are much more likely to get you the sale than barreling ahead with no regard to traffic lights.

Attitude, in my estimation, is a positive, affirming force. It makes every sale possible and every objection capable of being overcome. And what you'll find is that if you develop Attitude, you can find reinforcement for it from your client, and the client himself will become more positive as a result of your Attitude.

BELIEVE IN YOURSELF

5

It's all too easy, especially in a sales situation, to lose confidence in yourself. Believe me: It's happened to me more often than you might think. Because when you're confronted with a stubborn obstacle to completing the sale, nothing is easier than to think that the problem lies with you.

Years ago—a lot more than I care to be specific about—I was working to complete a sale. I'd done everything right: I'd asked a lot of questions, and I'd been responsive to the client's needs, focusing on what the client needed rather than what my company needed—all things that should have guaranteed smooth sailing toward that magic phrase: "I think we've got a deal."

Instead, nothing seemed to be going right. The client was grumpy and kept saying things like, "I just don't feel like we're connecting on a fundamental level." I was getting impatient at his inability to commit to basic, simple things such as price and delivery schedule. Every time I proposed something, he'd come back with something else.

At a certain point in the process I began to wonder: Is the problem with this guy the fact that I'm making my pitch badly? Am I not explaining the benefits of the service I provide? Is there something wrong with my approach?

Once you start questioning some small aspect of what you're doing, it's very easy for the lack of confidence to escalate. That's because, at least in theory, all the small decisions you make regarding how to structure a sale are linked to the larger decisions about the transaction. In other words, the very fact of your crisis of confidence is a sign that there's something good about the way you're thinking about the problem.

Of course, that's not much consolation under the circumstances. What you're thinking at the moment is more along the lines of, "I'm not getting through to this guy. He hasn't been understanding a word I've said for the past half hour. I guess it's because I'm not being clear enough in my explanation of the service's benefits. Or maybe I'm not showing him the dollars and cents advantages of the deal. Or maybe we're stuck because he's not seeing this whole thing in a long-term perspective and is concentrating just on the short-term benefits."

Now understand: *All of this may be true.* But that's not what's important right now. The biggest thing that's intruding into the sale right now is your lack of self-confidence. Until you get past that, you can't possibly hope to conclude things on an equable basis.

So here's what I want you to do:

1. **Stop circling.** Right now you're flying around in circles with your wings flapping frantically, not paying attention to where you're going as long as your activity level is high. This is a recipe for disaster. Stop it. Stop talking, stop pacing up and down, and sit quietly for a minute. Breathe deeply and concentrate on just one thing— something pleasant. It doesn't have to be sales-related. I just want you to get off the pattern you're on. Once you've envisioned that thing, spend a little time enjoying it. Examine it, touch it, smell it, and think about what need it gratifies. Right. You've completed that now. All

right, now come back to the present and the situation you're confronting.

2. **Break things up.** There's no problem so big that it can't be carved up into smaller problems. This approach is basic to problem-solving. Any issue can be divided into a series of discrete decisions, all of which you're capable of making. Once you start to think of the problem in smaller units, somehow it becomes much more easily solveable.

3. **Move the conversation forward.** One of the big sources of sales block is an inability of salespeople to get the conversation going in a positive direction. It's not that they don't know where it should go; it's that they can't figure out how to push it in that direction. But if you know what you want to talk to the client about, it should be a simple matter to turn your discussion with him down a positive path.

4. **Move past obstacles.** Bumps in the road are just that— bumps. They don't have to be giant roadblocks. But if you're convinced that *you're* the problem, it's all too easy to get hung up on an objection that may very well be minor. Your greatest aid here is your ability to separate small objections from large ones. For instance, a client may say that there's a big problem with delivery schedules. That's not a big problem; it's a small matter of working with your logistics people to find a logical, workable solution.

Each of these solutions starts with something basic: You've got to believe in what you're selling.

Here's where I think the problem begins. Too many sales-people buy into the somewhat cynical image of sales that's been promulgated by the media. They think that a salesperson is a sleazy individual with one hand on the customer's sleeve and the other on their commission. They want to counteract the idea that salespeople put their ethics in their back pocket whenever they start a pitch.

Are there salespeople like this? Yes, sad to say. But I don't believe for a minute that they're a majority of the profession. And I don't want you to think that either. Remember back to when you first got into sales. What did you think? That you were going to cheat people? Lie about your products? Steal bread from the clutching fingers of the poor? I don't think so. Insofar as you thought about what being in Sales meant, I'll bet you thought Sales was about giving people something they wanted for a reasonable price. And that's the absolute truth.

At the end of the day, sales success comes down to this: *You must believe in yourself. You must believe in what you're selling.*

SCENARIO

Let's look at what this would be like if you didn't believe in what you were selling:

> *Client*: Mr. Salesperson, I like what I'm hearing. You're telling me that this service will give me a guarantee of 50,000 widgets delivered on June 30 and with only a 5 percent additional cost for inventory expenses?

> *Salesperson*: Sure. Yeah. That all sounds good.

> *Client*: Great! Then I think we have an agreement. I'll ask our Legal Department to draw up the paperwork.

> *Salesperson*: Now before they do that, we should run over a few caveats. I want to cover all the bases, okay?

Client: Uh, sure.

Salesperson: Now, we should understand that the guaranteed delivery is only if there's a commitment on your part for 30,000 units for the following quarter.

Client: But wait, we—

Salesperson: You have to understand that we have to underwrite our costs, right? So that's only reasonable.

Client: Okay, but—

Saleperson: Suppose we say that the June 30 date is guaranteed with the understanding that there's some flex time on either side of that date. That the financial terms of the deal won't be altered if we go, say, ten or fifteen days either side of that date.

Client: We could look at some flexibility—

Salesperson: Great! I'll just suggest to our people that when they draw up the paperwork on this that we've agreed to a final delivery date of July 15. Now, I see that this is a Friday, so why don't we say July 18 . . . In fact, why don't we say July 20 as the firm delivery date, assuming that everything else works out?

Client: Well, I don't know.

Run over this scenario in your mind. Do you think the client is likely to be satisfied at the end of the day? Is he going to be willing to deal with your company in the future? Remember that you're in this for the long haul. And also remember that your client is going to remember—possibly longer than you—what kind of experience he had and how honest you were in your dealings with him.

Your integrity, which is at the heart of your abilities as a salesperson, rests on the question: How much do you believe in yourself? If you know your own strengths and weaknesses, and if you genuinely believe that the product or service you're selling will be of benefit to the client, you'll be able to present yourself to the client, or to anyone else, as a genuine, committed individual. If it's a fake, then that's how you'll come across.

In the scenario above, the salesperson was trying to pull a fast one on the client . . . and it showed. You need to keep in mind that your client isn't stupid; he's probably very intelligent, since he's made it this far in business. You should assume that he's going to understand what you're selling and be able to see how it will, or won't, benefit his business. So the important thing on your part is to be able to convince him that it will. Here are the strategies to help you do that:

1. **Know your product or service inside and out.** The more you know about it, the more you can believe in it.

2. **Keep a list in your pocket of the benefits what you're selling can have for your client.** Type this up before you call on the client and refer to it, if necessary, before you go in to see him.

3. **Constantly revise that list in light of the questions you ask your client.** As I explain elsewhere in this book, the key to good selling is knowing the right questions to ask.

4. **Keep telling yourself why you're a great salesperson.** I don't say this out of some 1960s California self-help guru nonsense; however, if you want to impress a client,

you first of all have to impress yourself. And the starting point is to understand what you have to offer.

All these things go back to a basic premise of positive selling: Success in sales comes from a conjunction of Attitude, knowledge, confidence, and a genuine concern with what kind of benefit you offer your clients. Once you get those elements lined up, you'll see deals come together.

BELIEVE IN
YOUR COMPANY

6

I have nothing but the utmost respect and admiration for the men and women who serve in the armed forces. Every day, these guys (both male and female) are putting themselves on the line. One of the things I've noticed in talking to people both in the services and those who are veterans is the immense pride they have in what they do. As a neighbor of mine, an ex-Navy guy, told me on one occasion, "There's two ways to do anything: the wrong way and the Navy way." I've heard similar sentiments expressed by others, whether in regard to the Air Force, the Army, or the Marines. Pride is a basic component of what keeps these organizations functioning.

This is more than just window dressing. Any student of military history—to say nothing of those who've actually served in the armed forces—will tell you that it's essential to have such pride and confidence in your organization because in a combat situation you've got to be sure that your comrades have got your back, from the staff sergeant all the way up to the four-star general. Any crumbling of that confidence and things can go very, very wrong indeed.

An outstanding example of this occurred during the Vietnam War. Soldiers at a certain point began to feel that the war was being fought for obscure political ends that didn't make any sense. They were being asked to risk their lives for ends that were unclear both to the folks back home and, often, to the politicians who had sent them there. The result, not surprisingly, was deterioration in morale and with it in fighting effectiveness. Some companies actually refused to go on missions. Other soldiers attacked their officers.

This was an extreme instance, but if you're a student of history you don't have to look far to see other cases where an army disintegrated because its soldiers lost confidence in their leaders. Napoleon's Grand Army of the French Republic in 1812 melted away on the historic retreat from Moscow. Thousands upon thousands of soldiers deserted and made their way home to France because they believed the army could no longer care for them and guarantee their safety on the march. On April 19, 1775, British soldiers retreating under fire from a clash with colonial Minutemen at Concord's North Bridge became a disorganized, panicked mob, running back to the safety of Boston.

DO YOU HAVE CONFIDENCE
IN YOUR COMPANY?

I bring these military examples up because I think one of the most important components of selling with a positive philosophy is that you've got to have confidence not only in yourself but in the organization you represent. This isn't at all the same thing as being a mindless cheerleader. I've met salespeople, on occasion, who confused having confidence in their company with being an apologist for it. The point is that if you believe your company has integrity and capability, you shouldn't have to apologize for it, at least most of the time.

A couple of years ago, when I was training a new company's sales force, I listened in on one of the cold calls made by a fairly new rep. I was struck by not just what he said but how he said it. Here's how the conversation went:

> *Salesperson*: We offer widgets that occupy a unique position in the marketplace, one that we think can be of real benefit to your company.
>
> *Prospect*: I don't know. There's a lot of people out there selling what you're selling. What makes you think you're different?
>
> *Salesperson*: Look, sir, I'm not going to spin a lot of stuff about our widgets being able to outperform others on the market by 75 percent. I'm happy to provide you with some figures about just what our widgets can do, but I don't think that's what makes us different. Let me ask you: If you could design an ideal widget, what would it do for you?
>
> *Prospect*: For a start, it'd boost our productivity and minimize product waste.
>
> *Salesperson*: How big a boost?
>
> *Prospect*: If we're just speculating, I'd say 50 percent.
>
> *Salesperson*: I can't promise you that. But I can promise that with our widgets you'll see an improvement in your time to market, and I'll work with you in every way I can to increase that productivity.
>
> *Prospect*: Why?
>
> *Salesperson*: Because when you win, I win. And when I win, my company wins. And that's important to me.

Note that last line. It makes a link that's extraordinarily powerful. To the degree that the salesperson is successful in solving his client's problems, he wins. His success is in direct proportion to the client's success. And when the salesperson wins, everyone in his company benefits.

This reflects the kind of team spirit that you find in well-functioning military units. All the members of the unit learn to depend on one another, and because of that, the team becomes more than the sum of its parts.

RELY ON THE OTHER MEMBERS OF YOUR TEAM

One of the sure signs of a poorly functioning sales team is when its members start to regard one another as the enemy. I've seen this in many companies; sadly, sometimes management even encourages it, in the mistaken belief that somehow this will increase the competitive spirit within the team and boost individual sales numbers. In some short-term instances it may have that effect, but the inevitable long-term impact is to drive down morale and with it sales numbers.

The best kind of sales teams are the ones where salespeople rely on each other, where they feel free to ask one another questions or offer advice. As in the military, where every soldier in a unit knows his comrades have his back, such teams are bound by a common spirit. They want to succeed, and they know every victory for an individual is a victory for the team. More than that, when an individual's accomplishments are reflected through the lens of team spirit, they become magnified.

This isn't just rhetoric; it's reality. I can tell you, for example, about a sales team I heard about from a colleague several years ago. When my friend first encountered them, they embodied the kind of cutthroat, *Reservoir Dogs* spirit I mentioned several paragraphs ago. Individual team members were barely speaking to one another, and it was common to give other team members misdirection and bad advice if salespeople somehow thought that would give them a boost within the department. It was a completely toxic atmosphere, and not surprisingly, sales numbers were starting to fall steeply.

Management was at its wits end in determining how to handle the situation—not least because it'd had a hand in creating it in the first place. My friend thought about the matter for several days and then came up with a solution.

The first thing he did was pull the team out of the field and send them on a team-building exercise. It wasn't one of those smarmy affairs where everyone sits in a room swilling coffee and talking about their feelings about one another. I have to say that I've never yet seen one of those kinds of exercises work.

No, this exercise was paint ball. The salespeople were formed into a team and sent into the field against another team, made up of the company's top managers. Under this pressure of people shooting paint capsules at one another, the salespeople rediscovered the value of cooperation. Of course, this wasn't before a number of them had been knocked out of the game. Paint balls, contrary to what you may have heard, can sting when they hit, so the lesson was a painful one, both literally and figuratively.

The teams came back from their day in the paint ball arena laughing and talking to one another. They joked about saving one another's rear ends and taking down management. Curiously, a highly competitive activity such as paint ball engendered a cooperative spirit, both within the sales team and management.

The second thing my friend did, several days later, was to start sending the salespeople on calls in teams of two. This was challenging, because two people on a sales call can easily start stepping on one another's toes. They can also intimidate the client and actually make the sale harder. But my friend felt these risks were worth it if it made the salespeople realize the value of cooperation.

It would be nice to say that the exercise worked in all cases. It didn't of course. There were some spectacular failures, and the team dissected these in review sessions held back at company headquarters. But for the most part, the salespeople on the team had positive experiences. They were able to see that each one, individually, could contribute something that improved the performance of the team. In two cases, the sales landed were substantially larger deals than had been expected when the salespeople first set up the client meetings. The salespeople discovered that in the course of their presentations to the client, they could play off one another's strengths and create greater energy than when just one person presented.

The system worked well enough that the company continued the policy, in cases where the salespeople thought it was warranted, of having two salespeople go on a call together. And, since in many cases these teams found their success rate improving, they didn't mind splitting their commissions because they came out ahead in the end.

My friend, who revisited the company six months later to evaluate how things were going, found something else as well. The sales team as a whole had a much greater sense of being part of the company. They took pride in its accomplishments and were glad to trumpet them to prospects and clients alike. This was because, as a result of their exercise in the paint ball field and with the sales teams, they could see that a well-functioning company can accomplish what individuals can't.

This is what I mean when I talk about the importance of believing in your company. When you sit down with a client, you should be firmly convinced that what you're selling is going to make her or his life better in some way. Believing in your company also means believing that your company has a future—that it's a growing, vital part of the corporate landscape.

Often this is easier when it's a new company. Ask any of the people who were there for start ups like Microsoft, Apple, or Google. These guys were garage entrepreneurs in a very literal sense. They worked crazy hours, often for very little money or for stock options that might, they hoped, turn into cash in the future. They did so because, above all, they believed in what they were doing.

It may be harder to evoke that kind of pioneering spirit in a company that's been around longer or one that doesn't see itself as on the cutting edge of technical innovation. But it's the responsibility of management to search for that spirit and to push it at every opportunity. In today's world, *everything is changing*. And that alone makes it an exciting and energizing time to be a salesperson.

BELIEVE IN WHAT YOU'RE SELLING

7

Contrary to the impression you may have gotten from this and other books of mine, I'm a very easy-going guy. I rarely get angry—at least in public—and I try to remain on an even keel in most of my personal and professional life.

There is, however, one thing that's guaranteed to get me going. That's if someone suggests that I'm lying or exaggerating.

I know I shouldn't rise to the bait, but it just bends me the wrong way. I've spent a great deal of my professional life building a reputation for honesty, and I hate to see anyone tear it down. The point was driven home to me recently in a conversation I had during a sales call.

I sell sales training. I've done it for a lot of years and, if you've read the blurb on the back of this book, you'll know that I've trained more than a quarter million salespeople. I'm proud of this blurb, but it's also just a cold, hard fact.

So it came as something of a shock when I'd finished a presentation to a board and the question came up: "Steve, can you show success for your methods?"

I was surprised, since the successful training of so many sales forces would tend to argue that I was doing something right, but I shrugged, accepted the question, and replied, "Sure. At Company X, after I was finished training, the company showed

Y percentage increase in recruitment of prospects. Gross sales increased during the following five years by—"

I was interrupted by a gentle chuckle from the VP of Sales. "Steve," he said, "I don't want to impugn your methods or your classes, but surely you don't interpret that percentage growth in sales solely to your training?"

I took a deep breath.

"Well," I said, "in fact I believe I can attribute a substantial amount of the growth to the use of my training methods. In fact, if I didn't believe that, I don't know why I'd be here."

Now I felt fairly launched. This is a theme that, over the years, has become very near and dear to my heart. I stepped out from behind the podium, holding the microphone and started to talk to the audience.

"The fact is," I said, "if I didn't believe in what I was selling to you guys, I wouldn't deserve to be standing here. You're experiencing growth because you're doing what I told you to do. That's the value I bring to this group. And that's the value I bring to *any* group of people I spend time with. The power of my belief is what keeps me going, and it's what should keep you going as well."

Now I knew I had them. They were interested and involved in what I was saying. So I forged on.

"Nobody you try to sell to," I said, "cares about you. Nobody cares about what you've done in the past. Nobody cares about who you are and what you've done. They don't care about anything except what they think you can do for them. And that's the way it should be. Your primary concern is the customer. If it's not, you need to re-think your line of work.

"So start from this customer-centric point of view. And ask yourself if the growth you've experienced is because your customers have become better customers . . . or because you've learned to sell to them better."

I waited for a response, and not surprisingly it was the one I expected. They recognized that they'd spent the past twelve to fifteen months not so much in polishing their sales technique but in educating the customer. They'd learned what the customer needed and wanted and they'd discussed how to provide it. At the same time, they'd learned to appreciate their product and how it would benefit the customer.

This is one of the most basic lessons of positive selling: You must learn to appreciate what benefits you bring to the customer with your product.

FOCUSING ON CUSTOMER NEED

How does this play out in real life? Let's consider the following scenario:

Mr. Executive: Quite frankly, Ms. Salesperson, I don't know why we're having this talk. There's nothing I can see that your product will do for us that isn't being done better and more efficiently by the Bambleweeny 31.10. Besides, it has lots of capacity for other functions that we'll need in the future.

Ms. Salesperson: Well, sir, I appreciate that, and I have to say that the Bambleweeny 31.10 is a fine product. But let me ask you this: What is the most important thing you need a computer to do *right now*?

Mr. Executive: At the moment, the main thing we need it for is to track the productivity levels of our employees in fifteen different countries and then find a common standard for comparison.

Ms. Salesperson: Mr. Executive, if you'll excuse my saying so, what you need a computer to do for you is well below the capacity of the Bambleweeny. You're using a cannon to ring a doorbell, and that's not an efficient use of computing power. I believe that our Calculex 800, which is cheaper than the Bambleweeny, will do the job for you more efficiently. And when you need to upgrade to a more complex level of function, we can make that change for you.

MAKE IT SPECIFIC

In this scenario, Ms. Salesperson has succeeded in focusing on the needs of the customer. She's not interested in selling him what he doesn't need; rather she wants to solve his immediate problem while explaining that her product will also be able to anticipate his future wants. This could well prove a decisive element in Mr. Executive's decision to purchase her product.

One of the points to learn here is that executives tend to deal in facts, figures, and visions that can be contained in numbers. Ms. Salesperson will have a very compelling case if she can put a dollar value on the function her computer system will play for Mr. Executive's company.

Mr. Executive wants to know in concrete terms what benefits this deal will bring to his workers. You could show him bottom-line stuff that would give him the idea of what probable economic growth can mean to his bottom line.

Positive selling means selling to *the actual needs and wants of the customer*. It doesn't mean trying to create a need that the customer wasn't aware of—and that's probably a false one. Rather, you have to pitch to the problem that the client is most aware of right now.

It's perfectly possible that at some point down the road Mr. Executive is going to want a computer with a more complex set of functions and programs than the Calculex 800. And if Ms. Salesperson can indicate to him that her product is adaptable to that, she'll more than satisfy his wants. But she needs to concentrate on the immediate problem, because that's what the customer is concerned about. The board, to which he answers, isn't interested in the problems of six months or a year from now; board members want to know what Mr. Executive is going to do for them today. Fortunately, with the aid of Ms. Salesperson's Calculex 800, he's got the answer.

Here, then, are the takeaways from all this:

1. **If you don't believe your product will solve the client's problems, the client certainly isn't going to believe it.**

2. **At the end of the day, what you've got to stand on is your integrity.** That means that you're going to have to be absolutely honest both with yourself and with the client. If you can't solve the client's problem, don't pretend you can, because the client will soon find out you can't.

3. **Solve future problems in the future.** For the purposes of your sales pitch, concentrate on the present. It's fine to let the client know that you've got the capacity to think about future challenges, but don't make them the focus of your pitch.

4. **Don't be put off by assaults on your facts and figures, but be sure you know what you're talking about.** You may well be facing a sophisticated client who knows the way to get a better deal is by undermining your confidence in what you're selling. Come to a sales call ultra-prepared.

THE POWER OF
INTEGRITY

8

Back in the mid-1970s, America was consumed by the Watergate scandal.

Those of you who are younger may find it difficult to grasp just how ubiquitous this thing was. Every night, television was filled with black and white images of the unfolding story. Senator Sam Ervin, the head of the Senate's Watergate Committee, called witness after witness to testify about the goings-on in the Nixon White House. The House Judiciary Committee, for the first time in more than 100 years, began officially considering the articles of impeachment.

Most dramatically, the Supreme Court heard the case of the tapes—the recordings Nixon had made of his meetings in the White House that he claimed he could not turn over to the special prosecutor in the Watergate case because it would destroy the integrity of the presidency.

The Court heard the case and the justices retired to their inner chambers to deliberate on an answer. Finally, on July 24, 1974, the Court ruled unanimously that Nixon had to turn over the tapes as possible evidence in criminal proceedings. There was a tense moment when people wondered if the president would obey a direct order from the Supreme Court. Then Nixon announced he would comply.

Seventeen days later, he became the first American president to resign his office.

THE MEANING OF INTEGRITY

The word "integrity" got tossed around a lot during the Watergate scandal, as it has during subsequent political imbroglios: Iran-Contra, Whitewater, and on and on. It seems sometimes as if the first thing everyone does when they're accused of wrongdoing in politics is make a statement to the effect that "I stand on my integrity."

Politics is usually a kind of selling, at least insofar as the candidates are trying to sell themselves to the public. But I don't want you to get the idea that the kind of integrity I'm talking about in this chapter has to do with the "integrity" shown by Nixon's henchmen in the White House in 1974. Or, for that matter, the "integrity" showed by Bill Clinton during the Monica Lewinsky scandal in the 1990s.

Integrity, as I see it, is a kind of honesty that penetrates you through and through. It influences everything you do as a professional. And for that reason, it's an essential component of positive selling. When you talk to a client, you're standing on your integrity because you're promising that your word is your bond. If you can't do that—if you can't speak the truth to a client—you're either working for the wrong company or you're in the wrong line of business. Any sale and its aftermath will eventually force any dishonesty on the part of the contracting parties to the surface.

This is one of the underlying lessons of Watergate and similar scandals. The people around the president who lied about their involvement in the Watergate burglary and its subsequent cover-up were making short-term decisions designed to protect themselves and their political capital. But truth, as someone said, is the daughter of time. With every day that passed, those lies became less and less tenable, until at last the whole rotten facade came crashing down on August 9, 1974.

Integrity, therefore, isn't just some nice Sunday school platitude to be hauled out for the annual report. In business, which exists on trust, it's basic. And if it's destroyed, everything can come to a smashing halt.

Go back and think about what I just said: Business is built on trust.

I know, I know. You're thinking: *Schiffman, trust has nothing to do with it. That's why we sign contracts—because we don't trust the other guy. We need everything spelled out in legalese to cover our behinds.*

It's true that contracts are a basic part of sales. But fundamentally, a contract gives structure to an agreement that you and the client have already made. The client makes that agreement with you because she or he trusts you to carry out your end of things. If you don't, the contract specifies various steps the client can take to obtain compensation for your failure to fulfill the bargain. But before the contract is signed, the client has made the agreement with you. In other words, the client relies on your integrity.

Think about Enron for a minute—a company that was built on a foundation of lies and evasions. The people who ran that enterprise were convinced they were, as one book about the affair has put it, "the smartest guys in the room." Maybe they were book smart; I don't know. But I know that in any meaningful business sense they were stupid. Because having destroyed their integrity, they can never get it back. If, by some chance, they ever try to start a business again, can you imagine any rational person wanting to sign a contract with them? Nope. Me neither.

SCENARIO

Think about the following scenario:

Salesperson: Let's just review. You need the units the second week of November, and because that's a rush for our facility, you're willing to pay a premium price of $1.30 per unit for the first 2,000 units. After that, the price goes back to $1.10 per unit.

Client: That's right. Now, can you guarantee delivery by the second week of November?

Salesperson: Yes. We'll make this a priority for our manufacturing team.

Client: I really, really need those units by the second week of November. If you miss delivery, it'll be very serious for me and knock a big hole in my budget.

Salesperson: I understand the importance of this to you. How about if we touch base every week for the next three weeks just to make sure we're staying on schedule? Maybe a weekly phone call every Thursday morning?

Client: Yes, that'd be good. I'd also like to write into the contract that if, for any reason, you fail to deliver the units by the time I need them, the price per unit will go down to $.80.

Salesperson: I'll have to clear a deal like that with my supervisors. That's a pretty serious financial commitment, and I don't know if we'd be willing to write something like that into the contract. I understand your concerns, and you're going to have to trust me, based on our ten-year relationship, that we'll do our job right and get those units to you. Are there any other steps we can take to make you comfortable with this schedule?

Client: Could I speak directly to the head of the manufacturing facility?

Salesperson: Again, I'll have to check on that. But I think that might be a possibility. We could probably set up a conference call for next week so you can explain your situation and make sure she understands why it's so essential to you that these units are delivered on schedule. Why don't I consult with my home office and give you a call tomorrow at 10 AM so we can discuss things?

Client: That would be great.

A couple of things to note here:

1. **The client is nervous—almost excessively so.** We've all had clients like this; sometimes it seems practically impossible to assure them that you're going to do what you say you'll do. It's important not to give up but to find out from them what would make them comfortable. At least that way they're the ones making suggestions.

2. **You have to avoid over-commitment.** The client here has asked for a major guarantee to be written into the contract. If, by some chance, something goes wrong at the manufacturing end, in addition to the cost of fixing it your company could be hit with a price guarantee that might well mean you'd actually lose money on these units. Don't agree to anything like that without talking to your supervisors.

3. **The salesperson makes an appeal to the client based on ten years of working together.** This is the real value of long-term relationships—they're the most important guarantee of your integrity. The longer you work with someone and the more consistently you meet their expectations, the more they're going to trust you when the going gets rough.

4. **The salesperson is specific in his suggestions and commitments.** Not just, "We'll call you every week to make sure we're on schedule," but "We'll call every Thursday." Specificity breeds trust. Of course, if you make a commitment like that, you'd better be sure you follow up on it. One missed call, and the whole structure of integrity you've worked to construct can come crashing down.

WHAT IF IT ALL GOES WRONG?

There are times—and if you're lucky, they won't be many—when despite your best intentions you fall down on a commitment to a client. It can be anything: a mechanical breakdown, labor troubles, political unrest, typhoons at sea. The point is, you're going to have to salvage your integrity from the wreckage.

The worst thing you can do is to ignore the situation. A colleague of mine from many years ago was faced with this kind of problem when he'd guaranteed delivery of a software package on a very aggressive schedule. His company rushed to get the product out the door, and the result was that it was buggy and slow. The Monday morning after it shipped (it had gone out of the warehouse the previous Thursday), he came into the office to find six messages on his phone from a very angry client.

Bob (not his real name) was a fairly level-headed guy, but he completely lost his cool after listening to the first message. He slammed the phone down and sat, staring at the blinking light, trying to collect his thoughts. After ten minutes, he went to try to pull himself together with coffee and a donut from the canteen. Then he listened to the other five messages, each angrier than the last.

He panicked and did the worst possible thing: He ignored the situation and turned to his other work. Every time the phone rang, he waited for Caller ID to make sure it wasn't the client.

The client did call several more times, leaving messages that escalated to shouting. Bob's inbox on his e-mail filled up with messages from the client, most of them in all capitals and speckled with exclamation points.

Halfway through the day, Bob was called into his supervisor's office. The manager was holding a sheaf of printed e-mails. Without preliminaries, he said, "I just got off the phone with [the client]. Want to tell me what's going on?"

We'll leave them there. Bob kept his job—barely. He was taken off that account, though, since the client had expressed a wish never to work with or hear his name again.

What should Bob have done?

The minute after he listened to that first message, Bob should have been in his supervisor's office, explaining what had happened and strategizing a response. By making his superior aware of the situation, he'd have been able to discuss the implications of the product's failure for the company as a whole and figure out how to handle what could, potentially, be a public relations disaster.

Once they'd agreed on a plan, Bob should have called the client, listened to the client's complaint, apologized, and offered possible solutions. Let's take these one at a time:

1. **Call the client.** Ignoring a problem like this won't make it go away. Rather, it'll make it much, much worse.
   The client's not going anywhere—he's simply going to escalate things (which he did, in this case, by calling Bob's manager). So get out ahead of the problem and call him. If you know in advance that there's a problem, call the client before he calls you. That will demonstrate you're genuinely interested in his business's welfare and want to figure out a solution to the problem you've caused.

2. **Listen.** The first stage of good customer service is all about listening. Be prepared for a long rush of comment and

complaint. Don't interrupt and don't, at this stage, offer explanations unless the client asks for one. What he really wants to do at this point is to talk. Talking through a problem can be therapeutic, and at this point he probably needs all the therapy he can get.

3. **Apologize.** Even if the problem wasn't directly your fault, apologize. Remember that you're speaking as a representative of your company, and you have to take responsibility for its actions. It will do you no good at all to say, "Well, it was really John down in Production who screwed this up; he's always messing things up. I hope they get rid of him soon." Apart from the danger of this remark getting back to John, it's not what the client wants to hear. He wants you to acknowledge that *you* (meaning either *you* the person or *you* the company) messed things up and created a problem for him. By apologizing, you implicitly take ownership of the problem and declare that you're the one who's going to fix it.

4. **Propose a solution.** This is where you lay out whatever you and your manager have come up with to address the issue. Offering a solution gets the conversation back on track in a positive direction. As always, keep the tone helpful and forward-looking, but don't commit to anything significant without consulting your supervisor. In circumstances like these, that's more important than usual.

Steps like that will maintain your integrity and show the client that you're mature enough to take responsibility for your own actions and those of your company. They also get you back on a positive track of fixing the client's problems, which is what sales should be about anyway.

SOME LESSONS
ABOUT DISHONESTY

9

Sadly, it's all too easy today to find examples of public and corporate dishonesty.

Let's consider the case of Congressman Anthony Weiner. Congressman Weiner was first elected to the House in 1999. He never got less than 59 percent of the vote in the seven terms he served in Congress—a remarkable achievement. An outstanding liberal voice in the House, he was seriously considered as a prospect for governor of New York, until 2011, when he was accused of sending lewd photographs of himself to various women.

When the accusations first surfaced, Weiner declared that his Twitter account had been hacked and that someone else had sent pictures from it. The pictures, he said, which did not reveal a face, weren't even of him. Then he stumbled, admitting that, well, they might be him, but he wasn't sure.

Questions kept arising, until finally Weiner admitted in a tearful press conference that he'd sent the photographs. He announced his resignation two weeks later.

Harking back a bit farther, consider the example of Richard Nixon. Among the most brilliant of foreign affairs-focused presidents, he was brought low by a scandal over the June 22, 1972, break-in at the Democratic headquarters in the Watergate hotel in Washington. For agonizing months investigations by Congress produced a dribble of admissions from his administration about how much he and his aides had known about the break-in and the extent to which they'd covered up their involvement. At last, in the face of congressional impeachment hearings and a Supreme Court order to release the contents of confidential Oval Office tape recordings, on August 9, 1974, Richard Nixon became the first American president to resign his office.

Maybe it's easier to find examples of dishonesty when you look among American politicians than it is in salespeople. I don't know. But what concerns me is that too few salespeople today appear to take away from these scandals one of the fundamental truths of selling, the one we explored in the previous chapter: At the end of the day, all you've got to stand on is your integrity.

This is more than a morality tale. There's a very practical aspect to it. When you sell to someone, you're making a promise. You're putting yourself on the line to deliver specific and quantifiable results. And believe me, you'll be held to those results. If you don't deliver, your phone will start ringing, and the client on the other end will want to know what's going on. So you'd better be able to justify what you've sold and whether or not it's doing what you said it was going to.

Using tricks to get out of this isn't going to work either. Of course, it's possible to use some sort of weasel-like legalese to stand on so you feel justified. But that won't last for long. At the end of the day, the client wants results.

SCENARIO

Let's listen in on a conversation between a salesperson and her client when the client has discovered that what the salesperson was selling is not all that it seems.

Client: I need to talk to you about the widgets you sold us.

Salesperson: Yes. If I recall, you took an order of 5,000 units.

Client: That's right. And you guaranteed that they'd be delivered by June 1.

Salesperson: Well, if you recall, what I said was that we'd do our best to see that they were delivered by that date. There are a lot of factors to be considered.

Client: Factors, shmactors! We didn't see those units until the 20th.

Salesperson: I'm certainly sorry about that, but I have to stand on the language of the contract. We didn't actually guarantee delivery by June 1.

Client: Your slowness led to a significant loss for us. I don't think we'll want to deal with your firm again, since it's clear that you had no intention of delivering on the date that was implied in your initial promise to us.

Here the salesperson is technically right—the contract didn't actually promise delivery of the product on June 1—but morally and practically wrong. The client needed the product by June 1, and if the salesperson couldn't guarantee delivery by that date, she should have specified so up front, and been very clear about it. That didn't mean she needed to lose the deal; there were lots of alternatives. For instance, she could have offered various alternate compensations if the deadline wasn't met. She could have worked out a sliding scale of price—that is, a certain discount for every day the product was late—which would have compensated the client for money lost due to delay. There are probably a dozen other things she could have done as well. The point here is that, sadly, her first instinct was to take a stand on the technical language of the contract.

THE IMPORTANCE OF LANGUAGE

Now, I want to make very clear that I'm a big advocate of clear, precise language in contracts. I've got lots of friends who are lawyers, and they constantly stress that the reason all that legal jargon appears in contracts is to protect both parties to the deal. Language is a peculiar thing—the philosopher William James said it is "the most imperfect and expensive means yet discovered for communicating thought"—and it's important that both you and the client agree on exactly what the agreement you signed promises.

Keeping that in mind, I want to stress that in many cases what's far more important than the language of a contract is its spirit. In the example I gave above, the salesperson is technically right. The language of the contract didn't absolutely guarantee delivery by June 1 (if it had, the client would be suing the salesperson's company for breach of contract). But the language in this case is irrelevant. What the salesperson has to respond to is the spirit of the agreement. The client needed those widgets by June 1. Since they've been delivered late, what can the salesperson do to rectify the situation?

I should note right off, by the way, that the first thing the salesperson should have done, when she knew the widget delivery was going to be delayed beyond what she'd indicated to the client, is call the client and discuss the situation. Virtually every circumstance is better if you know about it in advance, and the further ahead you know about it, the better the chance that you can do something about it.

But let's assume that the salesperson hasn't made this phone call and that this is the first time she's hearing about the problem. Here are my basic rules for positive handling of this unpleasant issue:

1. **Sympathize with the client's anger.** After all, this is costing the client money. Trying to make light of the situation

or passing it off as something that isn't very important is only going to aggravate things. The client is angry about your company's screw-up, and he wants to know that you're angry too. You don't have to scream and yell about the incompetent idiots in your shipping department, but make clear that you understand how serious the issue is.

2. **Ask for details.** This will help you resolve the problem as well as make clear to the client that you're taking it seriously and not looking for a simple answer. In the case cited above, you need to find out if any of the widgets the client received were damaged, if the people who made the delivery had any explanation of what caused the delay, and—a particularly important point—what dollar figure can be put on the problem.

3. **Ask for suggestions for what you can do to help.** (This doesn't mean you have to do everything the client suggests, but everyone appreciates their opinion being solicited.) Listen carefully to these suggestions and don't dismiss them out of hand. Make clear that you're as concerned as the client about how to clear up the problem.

4. **Don't make excuses.** The client doesn't want to hear, at this stage, that production was slowed by a strike at your manufacturing facility in Thailand or by storms and icy roads. This may all be true, but dwelling on it will just send a message to the client that your problems are more important than his. And he doesn't believe that.

Only when you've done these things is it appropriate to bring up the language of the contract and consider what guarantees have been made on both sides. It's possible, for instance, for the salesperson to say something along the following lines:

Salesperson: I'm really, really sorry to hear that the widgets weren't delivered on schedule. I'm sure that's made things difficult for you, and I'm sorry you suffered monetarily as a result. We certainly want to work with you to make things right. To begin with, I'd like, if we could, just to briefly review the language of the contract so I'm clear about the obligations we've incurred and how we can go about meeting them.

If you make suggestions about possible remedies to the situation, be sure they're just that: suggestions, not offers. You don't want to be put into a situation in which, under pressure from an angry client, you start making promises that your company can't meet. If necessary, it might be best if you took a list of suggestions from the client and then told him, "Well, these are all interesting, and I'll have to take them up with my boss to see which of them we could implement. How about if I get back to you tomorrow at 11 AM to continue this discussion?" This makes clear to the client that you're going to work on the problem and that you want to maintain your ongoing relationship with his company—both essential takeaways at this stage.

BETTER TO BE RIGHT? OR WIN?

It's easy for salespeople, when they run into a dissatisfied client, to become self-righteous; God knows, I've done it myself often enough to recognize the symptoms. It's particularly the case when the client is nasty about it.

A couple of years ago, I received a phone call from the head of a small company where I'd done sales force training. The session, as I recalled it, had gone well, and I'd come away with a good feeling about the salespeople getting a firm lock on what they were doing.

Thus it came as a considerable surprise to hear from the executive that he was furious with me. "You told me," he shouted into the phone, "that we'd see a 20 percent increase in our gross numbers! You guaranteed that!"

I knew myself and my contracts well enough to know that I'd guaranteed nothing of the sort. I started to say something, only to have him interrupt me. The way he sounded, I was surprised he didn't reach through the phone and shake his fist in my face. "We missed our numbers this month!" he howled. "What are you going to do about it?"

Every nerve in my body was telling me to shout something into the phone and slam it down. Somehow, by some miracle, I kept my temper. "Look," I said, "I want to help you, but we aren't going to get anywhere until you stop yelling. I want you to treat me with respect—the same way I treat you. If you do that, we can work together. Okay?"

There was silence for a minute, and then he grumbled, "Okay." And we moved forward.

Honesty about your product and your promises is the foundation stone of positive selling. At the end of the day, the client is relying on you to tell the truth and treat him with respect. If you do that, you can demand honesty and respect in return—and most of the time, you'll get them.

PUTTING THE
CUSTOMER FIRST

10

When I'm training salespeople, I like to sit and listen in on their calls. It gives me a good idea of their attitude, what they're prepared for, and how they approach a wide variety of situations. After all, there's nothing to make you think on the fly like being confronted with an unexpected question or challenge from a client.

SCENARIO

So one particular afternoon, I was sitting with a headset in my ear, listening as a salesperson pitched to a client.

> *Salesperson:* Could you tell me a little bit about what you think the main issue your company faces in the area of competition? (*Good,* I thought. *He's getting it right. The main thing is to find out from the client what his problem is.*)

> *Client:* Well, right now we're mainly concerned with fulfillment. Our main competitor has just installed a state-of-the-art warehousing system. When an order comes in, it's routed straight to the warehouse and goes to a team

of pickers. They can fill the order in under ten minutes. But for us, the system we've got in place takes an average of eighteen minutes, and that's compounded by a tendency to crash or spit out the wrong product when it gets overloaded.

(*Interesting,* I thought. *There's a real opportunity here, if the salesperson can seize it. What matters to the client is timing and accuracy in fulfillment. The salesperson needs to find out a bit more about this.*)

Salesperson: I think I've got just the product for you. It's a new warehousing software that will connect the warehouse with a server that can handle 15,000 orders per week.

Client: Well, that's impressive, but to tell the truth, our capacity at present is 10,000 orders a week, and we're really not ready to handle more than that.

Salesperson: Yes, but I can tell that the expansion of your business over the next year will increase your capacity. You need to look to the future. I'd really strongly recommend this system, since it'll not only solve the problem you've got right now, but it'll deal with your future expansion. And I think you'll find that the price is well worth it.

I took off the headset and rubbed my eyes. Wow! I thought. No wonder this place called me in. They've got trouble.

The issue here isn't the salesperson's lack of belief in the product. If anything, he's a bit too confident and too ready to dismiss the client's concerns and objections. The biggest problem is that he's more concerned about his own issues than those of the client.

Obviously, the sale of a large, expensive system means a big commission. And the situation might well be (and was, I found out later) that the company had encouraged its salespeople to push that particular system.

Here's what I would have done:

1. **Asked the client more questions about the fulfillment issue.** This is clearly the main problem he wants to solve, and it's a golden opportunity for the salesperson to step in with a solution that meets the client's needs.

2. **Found out more about what dollar value the client placed on that solution.** This is a fundamental of effective selling. You must know both the main problem of the client and how much the solution to that problem is worth to him.

3. **Tried to find out if the fulfillment issue was linked to other problems or questions.** This is a useful approach that salespeople too often ignore; whenever possible, find a product that solves more than one problem. You increase its value to the client, and an increased value means a potential increased price.

Above all, I would have held off on introducing a discussion of the solution until I knew more about the problem. This is another key tenet of positive selling.

Some people confuse positive selling with confidence. Confidence is part of the formula, of course; I've pointed out previously that you can't sell positively unless you believe in yourself, your company, and what you're selling. But that's just part of the trick. Another part is understanding the client's point of view. A third part is making the client's concerns the center of your sales pitch.

DRAMA

When I was much younger—*much* younger—I spent some time involved in amateur drama. It was an enlightening experience and, I think, helped me in my career as a salesperson and a sales trainer. I can't claim that I'm ever going to tread the boards on Broadway or the West End of London, but I think I'm better at my profession for the experience. There's a lot that salespeople can learn from actors, but one of the most important things is something a drama teacher said in a class I attended: Everyone wants something, and everyone wants something different.

Think about that. The world is made up of billions of individuals, each of them with a complex history of wants, needs, desires, and obsessions. Each of those histories is different. Moreover, people are a collection of wants. From the time we're born, we want things—from feeding and diaper changing up through the approval of our peers and into adulthood a decent income and a chance to grab a piece of the American dream. However—and this is a big point—the way in which we approach this dream is different.

The drama teacher's central comment was that drama arises from the conflict of different wants. My point is that a successful salesperson has to understand the individual needs of each of her or his clients. They're all unique, and they all have to be approached in a different way. Ignoring those differences and trying to find a one-size-fits-all solution will lead to disaster and ultimately to lost sales.

THE SCHIFFMAN SALES PHILOSOPHY

The title of this chapter is "Putting the Customer First." Just how do you go about doing that?

The Schiffman Sales Philosophy is pretty simple:

1. **Ask questions.** You can't possibly pretend that you care about the customer and his needs and concerns if you don't know what they are. So ask questions, and ask a lot of them.

2. **Don't assume that his answers will be the same as anyone else's.** In fact, you can be sure they won't. He'll have a unique set of issues, and you need to determine what they are and how you can provide a unique solution to them.

3. **Don't argue.** Get a sense of where the customer wants to go and follow along. There's absolutely no percentage in trying to argue with a customer about what he wants. He knows better than you do—or at least he thinks he does, and you're not going to convince him otherwise.

Remember as well that putting the customer first is not the same as putting the customer in control of the discussion. In fact, this is precisely what you don't want to do, since it means you've lost the initiative in the sales call. Some customers are very good at forcing this issue, seizing the initiative, and putting you on the defensive. Before you know it, you're explaining in great detail why you're asking the price you're asking, that you know it's unreasonable, and that you'll be happy to make some concessions.

It's essential that at all times you stay in control of the call. You can do this, interestingly, while not doing the majority of the talking. In fact, one of the valuable lessons you can learn as a salesperson is the power of silence.

Silence will do several things for you:

1. **Silence can be inviting.** Because we all have a tendency to want to fill a void, it will impel the client to keep talking— precisely what you want.

2. **Silent can be intimidating.** If you maintain silence, the client will think you're resisting his blandishments and be more inclined to give in.

3. **Silence can be disarming.** It says that you want the client to tell you what he wants. In other words, it goes a long way to convey precisely the impression that you want: You're putting the client first.

To put the client first is one of the most important principles in sales. Here are some things to remember about it:

1. **Putting the client first means finding out as much information as possible about him and his problem.** That means asking questions and encouraging him to talk. In a given sales call, the client should do 80 percent of the talking.

2. **Everyone's problems are unique.** Don't assume that your product will resolve the client's issues without discussing with him. Be willing to adapt what you're selling to the needs of the client.

3. **Use both silence and speech to invite the client to open up to you.** You want him to talk. The more he tells you, the better you'll be able to help him solve the problem and make a sale.

Once the client starts talking, you need to keep careful track of the things that are important to him. Just as important, you need to keep track of the order in which they're important.

SCENARIO

The sociologist Abraham Maslow developed a theory about what he called a hierarchy of needs. We establish that we need things in a certain order, and we respond to each other according to how well that hierarchy is being gratified. I wouldn't claim in any way to be an all-out devotee of Maslow, but I think he's got a point. Your client has a set of priorities, and the faster you understand what it is, the sooner you'll be able to respond to it and satisfy her or him.

For instance, imagine the following dialogue:

Salesperson: We can provide 5,000 widgets at twenty cents apiece by the end of next month.

Client: That's no good to me. We need the widgets in our distribution center at the start of the month or we'll miss the holiday season.

Salesperson: Would you be willing to pay a premium for early delivery?

Client: Yes, but only if there was a guarantee on the first 3,000 units.

Salesperson: Is the early delivery more important to you than the number of units guaranteed?

Client: I'd say they had roughly equal importance.

[Silence from Salesperson]

Well, if I had to choose . . .

[More silence from Salesperson]

I'd say we place more importance on delivery.

Okay, what's the hierarchy? It's pretty easy to judge from this exchange:

1. Delivery date

2. Guarantee

3. Price

In a real sales call, the number of factors is likely to be much higher, and the signs may be subtler. But whatever the case, you need to take careful note not only of what your client wants but of the order in which he wants it. That will be a significant element in how you negotiate and order the deal.

PART II
READY, SET, SELL!

ALIGNING YOUR GOALS WITH YOUR CUSTOMER

11

Some of you who are older—or possibly those of you whose parents read to them a lot when they were kids—may remember the story of Androcles and the Lion. (If you don't remember it, take a quick detour to Wikipedia and refresh your memory.) The story was also the topic of a play by George Bernard Shaw, but I remember hearing it as a little kid from my mother.

The story, in brief, is that Androcles, a meek tailor living in Rome during the first century A.D., was wandering around in the woods one day—when he came across a lion with a thorn stuck in his paw. Now, most people, seeing a lion in considerable pain and consequently with a short temper even for a lion, would have turned around and quickly walked the other way. But Androcles, who in addition to being meek, was very kind-hearted, bravely approached the beast and removed the thorn. The lion licked his paw several times, looked at Androcles closely, and vanished into the woods.

Several years later, during the reign of the Emperor Caligula, Christians in Rome were subject to persecution. Caligula had a large group of them, including our friend Androcles, rounded up and taken to the Coliseum, where, he decreed, they would be torn to pieces by wild beasts.

All of the Christians were naturally terrified, and when the gate of the arena opened and the wild animals entered, the Christians covered their faces in fear. And then . . .

Nothing happened.

The Christians looked up in astonishment. There was Androcles, and in front of him was the lion, from whose paw he'd plucked the thorn. The lion licked Androcles's face, and the other beasts, seeing their king refuse to kill the human, slunk away. Caligula was so astounded by this apparent miracle that he stopped persecuting the Christians, and they were allowed to worship in peace.

Well, that's the way I remember the story, at any rate. I'm sure there are variations on it. The point of it—as I'm sure you've figured out—is that doing a good deed today can reap rich benefits tomorrow. Another way of looking at it is that kindness will be repaid in the future with kindness.

DOES YOUR CUSTOMER HAVE A THORN IN HIS FOOT?

Figuratively, in this story, your customer is the lion with a thorn in his foot. The thorn, if you keep the analogy going, is whatever problem you're both trying to solve. What I'm saying here is that it's very much in your interest to pull the thorn out of his foot.

In other words, put the customer's needs above all else.

Scenario

I think it's important to make this point in a book devoted to creating a positive sales philosophy because all too often salespeople forget it. They focus on what's the most important thing for them and discount what the customer is saying. For instance:

Client: What's the guarantee of quality control per unit that you can give me?

Salesperson: That's not really the most important thing we should be considering right now. I think you're probably much more concerned with delivery schedule, since we could potentially run into the holidays, and that creates some disruptions for us.

Client: I am concerned about scheduling, but—

Salesperson: Suppose we push our delivery date out by two weeks, which gives us time to play around with the schedule a bit?

Client: I don't think that works very well for me.

Salesperson: Obviously a quicker delivery date is preferable, and I understand that, but it's not going to do you a bit of good if our people can't meet it, is it?

Client: No. Could we go back to the—

Salesperson: Let's take the schedule I suggested as the basis for discussion and go from there.

Client: Okay.

Since, in the end, the client has accepted the point that was very important to the salesperson—extending the delivery schedule—you might think in this exchange that the salesperson and her company have come out the winners. But you'd be wrong.

There should be a special circle in professional hell for salespeople who interrupt when a client is speaking. I can't think of any reason for doing so, and this salesperson has done it twice in one minute. Moreover, she's clearly not concerned about what the client wants to talk about, which is the issue of quality control. All she wants to discuss is what's important to her—the schedule.

It's quite possible that she's right in assuming that the issue of the schedule is of greater importance to the client's interests than the question of a QC guarantee. But that's irrelevant. The point is, *What does the customer want to talk about?* If it's QC, then the best thing is to resolve that point before moving on. In fact, if the salesperson can resolve the QC issue quickly and efficiently, it builds the client's confidence that she can solve the knottier problem of the schedule in a way that's not going to adversely affect his company.

In other words, the salesperson, by putting the client's concerns first, is more likely, not less, to get concessions out of him that are important to her. In the same way that our friend Androcles acted selflessly and later benefited from it, so a salesperson who focuses on the client is going to reap rewards later on.

THE MAIN POINT OF A SALE

I've said this before, and I'll continue to repeat it throughout this book: The point of a sale is to solve a problem for the client. Every client has a problem (or, in fact, a series of problems) for which she or he is looking for a solution. If this weren't the case, the client wouldn't be talking to you. Potentially, you have a product or service that can solve that problem. But first, you've got to find out what the problem is.

This process represents something of a challenge, because the client herself may not be aware of the scope and nature of the problem. It may start as something very simple—"I need a better supplier of widgets"—and extend to a much more significant issue—"I need widgets that ensure I have repeat customers."

The only way to find out the customer's problems is to ask her about them. Of course, you can and should do research before the sales call, which can give you a general idea of the problems the industry and the client's company probably are encountering. But only the client can tell you what she *thinks* her problems are. Once you've found that out, you can start solving them.

That's why, for thirty years and more, the foundation of the Schiffman sales method has been this simple proposition: Ask your clients questions to get the sale.

It's amazing to me how many salespeople fail to understand this idea. They think that the proper function of salespeople begins and ends with persuading people to buy something. There's an element of persuasion in sales, of course; it would be silly to pretend there isn't. But the force of your persuasive technique lies in the fact that you are focused on the client's interests and finding out how they align with your interests. That is, how can you create a deal from which you both benefit?

This is called Enlightened Self-Interest. You're acting in a way that will benefit you, but it also benefits the client. The minute you start to remove the client from the equation and focus just on you, everything goes out of balance.

Think about the scenario we considered above. The client, once she sits down and really thinks about the situation, will realize that not only does she still have no guarantee of quality control per unit, something she believes is important, but she's also agreed to an extension of the schedule, which probably has implications for the rest of her business. It's possible that she'll go ahead with the deal, but it'll leave a sour taste in her mouth. The next time she sees you, she'll be thinking, "He put one over on me the last time we talked. I won't let him do that again."

And your next negotiations will be harder.

WIN BY NOT FIGHTING

Centuries ago, the Chinese military theorist Sun Tzu wrote a classic work about strategy, *The Art of War*. In recent years it's been extensively studied in the West, not only by military theorists but by business people. That's because Sun Tzu's ideas have a great deal of application to the modern business world. (Sun Tzu's ideas have also been applied to everything from innovation to dating. The old boy would be very surprised at what happened to his book over the centuries.)

One of Sun Tzu's propositions runs, "To fight and conquer in all your battles is not supreme excellence; supreme excellence consists in breaking the enemy's resistance without fighting." In other words, it's much better to get what you want without fighting than to have to battle the enemy for it. This applies to sales as well as to the rest of business practices. Fighting with your client is exhausting and, ultimately, not very productive. It's much better, if possible, to follow her lead, go where she wants to go in the discussion, and find areas of agreement where you can do deals. If she wants to talk about QC . . . all right, let's discuss it and work something out. Then, at our leisure, we can come back to the question of schedule.

If, by some weird happenstance, the client doesn't bring up the schedule, bring it up yourself once it's clear she's put everything on the table that's of concern to her. Maybe she hasn't thought about it. Maybe she's waiting for you to bring it up. Maybe she thinks it's already settled. Who cares? Take the initiative and raise the point, but only when you're sure she's ready to discuss it.

Sales can, of course, be like warfare. You're trying to conquer territory, win concessions, and hold the positions you've won. But it's a strange sort of warfare, because you also want your opponent to benefit from the battle. So don't always think that your objective has to be to win a crushing concession from the client, one that she'll regret later on. Put her interests first, and help her to understand how what you're selling is of benefit to her. Just as was the case with Androcles and the lion, this sort of approach will come back to you with considerable benefits.

I have a vague recollection that after the events in the arena, the Emperor Caligula gave Androcles gold coins. Androcles and the lion made the rounds of the city, and people came out of their houses to stare at them in amazement.

I wonder whatever happened to that book my mother used to read that story from . . .

DO YOUR
RESEARCH

12

I well remember the first time I signed onto the Internet.

For months—actually for probably a couple of years—I'd been hearing about this thing. I wasn't too clear about what it really was. It sounded as if someone had linked a bunch of computers together for some strange purpose and then turned the whole thing on, hoping for the best. Gradually, it became a little clearer to me. The Internet was a way that computers around the world could communicate with one another. There was this system called the World Wide Web that had a lot of places you could go—called websites—and these places had information.

Finally, I took the plunge. I signed up for one of the then-available services, probably AOL, and plugged in my username and password. There was an agonizing wait (people today forget how slow the Internet load-time was in the early days) and then the home page finally came up.

I sat entranced. I felt as if a whole new world had just opened at my fingertips. And it had.

Today, we accept the Internet as a fact of life. Now that Google has become a common verb, it's hard to remember what things were like as little as fifteen years ago. Now, if I want some basic information about something—a date, a name, and so on—I've got dozens of sites, starting with Wikipedia, that I can go to and find out. Fifteen years ago, we had reference books and libraries that we constantly consulted.

Fifteen or twenty years ago, researchers consulted tools like the *Reader's Guide to Periodical Literature*, an annual index to major magazines and journals. We checked business sources like the *Business Periodicals Index* and *Standard & Poor's Index*. Today these resources, insofar as anyone uses them, are online, available with a couple of keystrokes.

I bring all this up because one of the most irritating phenomena I see today among salespeople is a tendency not to do their research before calling on a company. And I can see no excuse whatsoever for this.

It isn't as if research is all that hard. It requires you to sit down in front of your computer, have a clean pad of paper on which to take notes, and have the ability to search for a set of words and phrases that are going to clue you into what your target client does to make money. How difficult is that?

One of the reasons I suspect that some salespeople neglect this basic step of successful selling is because, they say, it can be time consuming. When I hear this, I have to smile. Time consuming! They should have tried it in the old days, lugging through copies of the *Reader's Guide*, pouring over back copies of annual reports and financial statements—often printed on yellowing paper and smelling faintly of fading ink and withered librarians. Research today is twenty, fifty, a thousand times faster and easier.

Nonetheless, I'll admit to the truth of what one of my old college professors once said: There's nothing more inefficient than research.

But it's absolutely necessary. You've got to know the facts about a company before you can sell to it. So what, in your research, should you be looking for?

Here are some thoughts:

1. **Start with the basics.** You need to know the who, what, where, when, and how about your client. Who are they, what do they do, where are they located, when were they

founded, and how do they go about fulfilling their corporate mission? Chances are you'll find the answers to some of these questions in the company's annual report (though keep in mind that since the annual report is crafted for shareholders and the public, it may not be entirely candid).

2 **Find out the names.** You're not selling to an abstraction called the X Corporation. Your presentation will take place before flesh-and-blood individuals. They have interests and goals, hopes and dreams. Above all, they've got a history with the target company. A search of newspaper and magazine articles can give you some valuable clues about who these people are and what might be productive approaches to them.

3. **Determine needs.** Every company needs something. This is Sales 101, but too many times salespeople forget about it. You're selling to the company because it needs something. If it didn't, it wouldn't need you to sell to it, and you wouldn't be sitting there. So your first, number one priority is to find out what the company needs. Most of the time, you'll have to ask questions to determine this. But your pre-call research will give you an idea of what questions to ask.

4. **Pay attention to big events.** You're going to sound like an ill-informed idiot if you don't know about big things that have happened to the company or to the individual you're talking to. Some things to watch for include:

   - Promotions

   - Reorganizations

   - Acquisitions/mergers

   - Significant financial difficulties/bankruptcies

   - Change of locations

3. **Determine rivals**. Companies exist in a state of constant competition. Their competitors are likely to generate some of their biggest needs and problems, ones you're being called upon to solve. So find out who their rivals are and what advantages or disadvantages these companies have over your client.

ORGANIZE YOUR RESEARCH

Once you've spent some time on the Internet exploring your company—which should include a visit to the company website and to those of its main competitors, you'll have pages of notes about them. You need a way to have this information at your fingertips during the sales call without being overly obvious about it.

These days, in the high-tech age in which we live, I don't see anything wrong with taking a laptop computer to a sales call. In fact, it may be expected, since the people you're talking to are going to be pretty high-tech as well. This makes life a lot easier for you.

Make a file on your desktop for your client company. Label it with the name of the company (keeping in mind that during the sales call, it's possible that your client or someone affiliated with her may see your desktop and therefore see the names you've assigned to different files).

Within the file, create a series of separate files with labels such as:

- Background

- Officers/organization chart

- Product strengths/weaknesses

- Competition

- Facts/figures

Most important, create a file with a name such as "(My product/service)—Benefits." This is the most important file you'll access during the sales call, because it's the one that will tell the client how your product or service can solve her problem. This is probably the file in which you want to keep your PowerPoint presentation (or whatever other form of presentation you've created).

SOME THINGS TO REMEMBER
ABOUT RESEARCH

1. **Your client already knows a lot of the material you've researched, so there's no need to repeat it.** There's nothing more irritating than having to sit through a talk by someone who's determined to tell you things you already know. I've had some painful experiences in this regard. I once watched an inexperienced salesperson wade through a twenty-minute presentation to a client on the history of the client's own company—despite the fact that the client to whom he was presenting was the founder of the company and knew its history better than anyone else. None of that mattered to the salesperson; he had done his research, by God, and he was determined that he was going to get if off his chest or die trying. The client sat in his chair, sinking lower and lower, looking by turns bored and irritated, and the salesperson recited facts and figures that were completely irrelevant to what he was trying to sell. Needless to say, things didn't end well.

2. **Your organization of facts reflects the level of professional service you'll provide.** If the client sees you fumbling around to find information, he'll assume, quite rightly, that this is how you normally operate. There's

nothing less impressive than someone who can't lay his hands on a piece of needed information. This is why I recommend having the folders handy. If you don't bring a laptop to the proceedings, I still recommend folders—physical ones, neatly labeled, possibly color coded, but in any case with the information you'll need organized in a readily accessible form.

3. **The strongest and most effective information is new.** Your client may know a lot more about her company than you do, but you've had the opportunity to view her company in a broader context and, I hope, with more time for research. The biggest impression you'll make on her is when you tell her something she didn't know before. Often this is about the competition, but sometimes it may be gleaned from news reports, obscure sources, or your own knowledge of the industry. The information may be factual or it may be a new insight that gives her a different perspective on what she's trying to accomplish. In any case, don't waste your time telling her things she already knows. Look for something she doesn't know.

4. **Research is just a path to asking questions.** No matter how long you've spent glued to a computer screen, finding out everything that's been written about the client's company, there's always more to learn. And the best source to learn it from is the client. The purpose of your research, aside from anything else, should be to guide you in knowing what questions to ask. Every answer you get goes into those invaluable folders. Since you anticipate having a long-term relationship with this client, all this information is future gold in sales calls.

Finally, I have to caution you to look at all research with a critical eye. Again, remember that the ultimate authoritative source is the client—at least most of the time. Clients occasionally don't know what they're talking about and your research may prove them wrong. If that's the case, be gentle about it, but firm. No one likes to hear they're wrong, but they'll probably appreciate it if you can show how the correct information brings whatever problem they have just that much closer to a solution.

FIRST IMPRESSIONS COUNT

13

Back in 2009, I had set up an appointment to meet someone who was going to help me with my books. We scheduled a meeting at a hotel, planned for breakfast at 9 AM sharp. I told him in the confirmation e-mail that I had another meeting at 10:30 AM, so this would give us plenty of time to chat, have a leisurely meal, and for me to get to my next meeting.

It's been my experience that it's wise to show up to a meeting a bit early, so at 8:55 AM I was at the entrance to the hotel dining room. At 9:10 AM the hostess approached me to ask if she could seat me. I declined, feeling a faint rumbling low in my stomach. At 9:15 AM I gave into the inevitable and said to the hostess, "I'm afraid I've been stood up. Perhaps you could seat me."

I'd barely made it to my table when the fellow I was meeting barged into the dining room. As he strode up, I could see other guests surreptitiously glancing at him. This wasn't surprising.

His hair was uncombed and stood straight up on his head. His shirt was half tucked in, and he had no socks on. He looked, in short, as if he'd woken up ten minutes ago and staggered downstairs for our meeting—which I subsequently learned was the case. I felt deeply embarrassed that I was responsible for bringing this scarecrow into the dining room, but there wasn't anything to be done. I greeted him, and we sat down.

From there, everything just got worse.

He made a ham-handed attempt to flirt with the waitress, one that was decisively rejected. He chewed with his mouth open, spewing a steady stream of food particles over his shirt. He complained about the food, the service, the hotel, and the weather in tones that could be heard in every corner of the room. I felt myself slowly shrinking down into my seat, hoping against hope that the end of this meal would come into sight.

Finally, the check arrived and we stood up. He offered a clammy hand and said, "Well, Steve, I enjoyed this. I'm looking forward to working with you."

I made a hasty excuse and beat a retreat. I don't need to tell you that at the first opportunity I broke off my working relationship with him.

But here's the curious thing. I read books that he'd edited or written and spoke to publishing professionals who'd worked with him. They all affirmed that his books were brilliantly written and cleanly edited and that he hit every deadline and was completely professional in all his dealings with them. After listening to enough of this, I began to wonder if I'd made a mistake in not hiring him.

THE FIRST FIVE MINUTES

I concluded, ultimately, that I hadn't made a mistake. This man confirmed a rule I made a long time ago: If I don't like someone in the first five minutes, there's probably a good reason for it. Over the years I've occasionally had reason to question this rule, but not very much. Most of the time, it holds up pretty well.

First impressions are essential. They're what stays with us, because they tell us so much about a person's character. Of course, it's possible to catch someone on an off day, when everything has gone wrong, from their breakfast to what they read in the paper over their morning coffee. But even so, I maintain that someone's true personality comes out almost immediately, despite the circumstances.

This was confirmed to me a while ago by a story I heard about a sales call. The rep, a relatively experienced salesperson, called on a new prospect. He pulled up his car at the company, walked in and identified himself to the admin, and asked about his appointment with Mr. Smith, the CEO of the company. "He'll be with you in a moment," she replied, continuing her task of watering a large bunch of lilies sitting on her desk.

A moment later the rep was introduced to Mr. Smith. More precisely, Mr. Smith came staggering out his office door, convulsed with sneezes, and knocked the sales rep base over apex. The two crashed to the ground, and Mr. Smith, continuing to sneeze uncontrollably, clawed at the rep's arm.

"Do something!" he croaked.

The rep, thinking quickly if not logically, grabbed the nearby pitcher of water with which the admin had been nourishing the lilies, and emptied it over Mr. Smith's head. There was a loud splash, a squeal of astonishment from the admin, and a pathetic "Glub!" from Mr. Smith.

The rep, figuring this was where he went back to the office and reported failure, got to his feet, expressed his apologies in a few heartfelt words, and started for the door.

"Wait!" yelled Mr. Smith. "Where do you think you're going?"

The rep paused, his hand on the door handle.

Smith shook himself like a St. Bernard and said, "That's the smartest thing I've ever seen anyone do. I felt as if my head were coming off, and now I don't have to sneeze at all. If you can think on your feet like that, we need to talk!"

I don't know if I would have reacted like the rep did. But the point is that he proved himself someone capable of quick, innovative thinking. Just what you'd want in a sales rep.

THE BEST IMPRESSION

Positive selling is all about believing in yourself. And that means that you've got to project a strong, positive image toward your clients. Hopefully, none of them will be sneezing convulsively and you won't have to empty a pitcher of water over them. Whatever the case, though, your most important priority in the first five minutes of a sales call is to project a lasting impression of confidence, competence, and concern.

Confidence. It's important to distinguish between confidence and over-confidence. Confidence says you can do what you've promised and are willing to stand behind your results. Over-confidence says you don't really know what you've promised, and you're pretty sure you won't be able to deliver so you'll compensate by promising even more. There's no more sure way to undermine the trust of a client than to promise and then fail to deliver. On the other hand, if you tend to under-promise and over-deliver, it builds confidence in you.

Competence. When you say what you'll do and you do what you said, you have competence. It's not just about the technical skills of your profession; it's about attitude. For instance, if you tell the client that you'll call him on Tuesday to make sure the product was delivered to his warehouse, you'd better make sure you call on Tuesday. Calling Wednesday morning means you found something that was of greater priority than him, and no client wants to hear that. Competence is about following through and paying attention to details.

Concern. If you put the client first, you're displaying concern. Too many salespeople are inclined to focus on their needs or the needs of their company. They worry about meeting their commission or hitting quotas. I'm not suggesting that you don't keep these things in mind; your career will quickly go south if you don't. I'm just saying that it's best to let the client know that he and his problems are uppermost in your mind at all times.

It's important to make a strong first impression on the client and at the same time establish control over the situation. Acknowledge his importance. The client wants to feel respected by you. Above all, he wants you to understand the importance of his time. Don't waste it.

SETTING THE TONE FOR THE CONVERSATION

14

Let's just imagine it.

Your cab at the airport was late. You didn't sleep well the night before. You've got a splitting headache—one of those ones that feels like two jackhammers are pounding at alternate sides of your brain, trying to see who gets there first.

The last thing in the world you want to do is to sell. And yet . . .

And yet, your client is looming in front of you. Some part of you is saying that if you can just pull off this sale, you'll be set. This is the one. The big one.

So you pull yourself together and all the basics come running back. You remember to do only 20 percent of the talking during the interview, ask lots of questions, and keep your client's needs at the forefront of the interview.

But somehow—you don't know how—it all feels wrong. Before you know it, you're in a cab headed for the airport and wondering where on earth your sale went.

START THE CALL RIGHT

I don't wake up especially well in the morning. As a rule, I've got to spend a little time wandering around, getting coffee together, picking up the paper and glancing at the headlines, and poking my head through the curtains to see what the weather's doing. Once I've done all that, then, and only then, am I ready to join the human race.

Some people take even longer. A friend of mine has told me that he doesn't feel he's fully woken up until he's on his way to lunch. Other people have their morning routines, all of which are designed to get them up and running on a full tank. All of us, in other words, like to get our day going right. Our habits, formed over a lifetime, are all intended to make us feel secure and positive by the time we've actually got to get down to the business of interacting with other people.

Sales calls aren't necessarily that different. There's a routine to them to get them off on the right foot. We all have our own style, of course, but here's what I do when I'm meeting a client for the first time:

1. **Get to the call a few minutes early.** This will give you a chance to run over the notes for your presentation, relax, and get the lay of the land a bit. Also, if necessary, you can use the bathroom facilities. You don't want anything to interrupt your presentation.

2. **Greet the client with a firm handshake and a smile.** If you're in any sort of gloomy mood, this isn't the time to show it. (For reinforcement, read Chapter 4 in this book.)

3. **Once you've gotten to the place where you'll be presenting, lay out your notes in front of you for easy access.** There's nothing more annoying during a presentation than someone fumbling around in her or his

briefcase for an important piece of paper. Ask for a glass of water, or bring your own water bottle with you. If you prefer coffee, ask for a cup—anything to keep your throat in working order.

4. **Ask the client to tell you about the company.** Of course, most of this will be familiar to you since you've done your research, but it's a good way of learning how the client sees what she does, as opposed to the way other people see it. Her comments may give you some insights; they'll certainly give you the opportunity to start asking questions. And they establish the tone for the call—you want the client to do a lot of the talking and you want the conversation to be a mutual exchange, not just a presentation on your part.

If you've met the client before, the last point in particular changes. In that case, you want to ask about the company and the industry—what's changed and what's encouraging. Then, and only then, turn to the question of the problems the client has encountered recently.

In my experience, clients are more than willing to talk about problems. These are what consume most of executives' time, so it's natural that they loom large in their thinking. The bad thing, though, about starting a discussion with problems is it puts the conversation in a negative light.

Three years ago, I met a client over lunch. It was a nice day, the restaurant was one of my favorites, and I was feeling pretty good about life. We ordered lunch, and I leaned back in my chair comfortably.

"So. How're things going?"

"Okay, I guess."

"How are you guys being affected by the economy?" (This was right about the time in 2008 when Wall Street was experiencing its first big wave of panic.)

He sighed. "Well, things are pretty awful. None of our products are working. Sales are down across the board."

I took a sip of wine to fortify myself. "Can you tell me what *is* working?"

"Nothing."

"Anything that's performing better than the other product lines?"

"Nope."

It went on like this through the whole lunch. By the end of it, I was ready to walk out into Union Square and shoot myself. I hadn't been able to uncover a single bright spot, and even though we'd agreed on a follow up meeting the next week, I had a sneaking suspicion it would go the same way.

Hindsight is 20/20, of course. In thinking over the matter later (over a stiff drink; well, I had to do *something* to recover from the lunch), I realized that the biggest mistake was leading with the economy. This was 2008, remember, when Lehman Brothers collapsed and the stock market plunged. The client was feeling gloomy. After all, who wouldn't? So my job, to get the tone of the conversation right, was to find some piece of positive news, anything, to push the thrust of the discussion in another direction.

Bad emotions, like good ones, tend to build upon one another. In Chapter 4 on Attitude, I suggested that we get part of our positive Attitude from the strong emotions we evoke in an audience. But this can work the other way around as well. Once the client started to talk about everything that was wrong with his business, any bright spots I could see on the horizon faded into the distance. Gloom and doom were everywhere, as far as I could see. For the life of me, I couldn't think of anything positive to say.

Afterwards, when I'd had time to think about it, I realized there were quite a number of good things I might have brought up. But the negativity of the client's mood infected me as well.

TURNING THINGS AROUND

Especially in a time of economic downturn, when you're afraid to go to the business pages of the web for fear of what they're going to say, sales calls can get sidetracked in the way I just described. So what can you do, if that happens, to change the tenor of the discussion?

Here are some alternatives:

1. **Break off the call.** If you're in danger of talking each other so far down that a sale will be impossible, one possibility is to call it a day and come back later. That option is better than losing the sale, since it gives both of you time to recover and offers you a chance to think out a detailed strategy for selling to someone who's not inclined to buy. (For more on this, see my book *Selling When No One Is Buying*.) It's amazing what a difference in mood a couple of days can make.

2. **Change the subject.** This is less drastic than ending the call completely, but it can be just as useful. On one or two occasions when a sales call has been seriously imploding, I've scratched the depths of my memory to recall anything I can about the person I'm talking to. On one occasion, I blurted out, "Oh, I just realized your daughter's getting married next month. How's the planning for that going?" Sure enough, the prospective father of the bride brightened up and stopped thinking about how bad his business was and concentrated on how much he was looking forward to the wedding day. When we returned to the subject of the call twenty minutes later, the tone had shifted dramatically, and I was able to put the sale across.

3. **Look for a piece of positive news.** If the client is hell-bent on telling you how bad the industry is these days, think of

something good to say about it. It can be anything: news of a significant technological breakthrough, an interesting idea for marketing, and so on. But the important thing is to shift the tone from negative to positive.

The effect of each of these strategies is to stop the tendency of bad news to build on bad news. Once you've put an end to that rhythm, you can plot out how to get the call back on track.

WHAT ELSE AFFECTS TONE

Sometimes it's not even bad news about the industry or the business that can drain energy from a sales call. Sometimes it's something simple: the weather, what the client had for breakfast, how his favorite sports team is doing. A friend of mine from the Boston area has told me that when the Red Sox are losing, the whole town turns sour and gloomy. I'm from New York, so I have to think that's a good thing (apologies to any Red Sox fans reading this), but I know what he means.

You can't control the weather or your client's eating habits (to say nothing of his taste in sports teams), but you can take those into account when planning the opening of your sales call. If the weather's gray, find something else cheerful to talk about. (Another friend of mine, this one from the Seattle area, has said on occasion that if he allowed the weather in the Pacific Northwest to influence his sales pitches, he'd never sell anything.) If the client looks queasy or tired, talk about an interesting piece of local news you heard that morning on television—anything to engage him and get him to perk up.

A favorite author of mine, P.G. Wodehouse, once wrote that the way to someone's heart is through their hobby. I've found over the years that it's very helpful to know what interests outside of business your clients have. What are they into? Sailing? Running? Sports? Home repair? If you find that an important client is a fanatic about stamp collecting, I suggest you do some serious research into philately. You don't have to become an expert—just knowledgeable enough to carry on an intelligent conversation. In the event that sales talk turns gloomy, you've got something to turn to that you know will pique the client's interest and get the enthusiasm meter running again.

ESTABLISH THE PACE

15

Several months ago, I had dinner with a group of family members, including my grandnephew, now aged eleven. I hadn't seen him for a while, and typically, while my back was turned, he'd grown about three feet. After I told him it was good to see him and asked some preliminary questions about school (which he answered with a muttered, "Okay, I guess" and "Yeah, pretty much"), we sat down to dinner. I was placed next to him, and on the other side was another kid about the same age—the stepson of another relative.

As boys do, these two were initially suspicious of one another and confined their conversation to quick, sideways glances and an occasional grunted remark. But pretty soon, at least in part as a defensive alliance against the adults at the table, they began to talk in low voices. After a minute or two, they turned partially away from the table to face one another.

Then the talking *really* began.

I found myself listening to the line of chatter and marveling both at the subject matter—which was video games, pretty much a sealed book to me—and especially at the speed of the discussion. They sounded as if they were stepping on one another's words, but each knew exactly what the other had said and had his answer on the tip of his tongue. There were times when to my tired old ears, it sounded like a foreign language. I tried to listen, to grasp some thread of the topic that I could tug on.

"So," I said finally, "these are computer games you're playing?"

The conversation stopped dead. You'd think I'd dropped a rock into the middle of it. Both boys slowly looked at me, and then my nephew, speaking very slowly and clearly said, "No, Uncle Steve. This . . . is . . . for . . . the . . . *PlayStation*." He looked at me anxiously, evidently wondering if he'd gone too quickly for my enfeebled understanding. I nodded and withdrew to my dinner while the two boys, relieved that I hadn't said something even more embarrassing, resumed their talk.

At the time, I was amused by my failure to enter into a technological discussion conducted by a couple of boys fifty years my junior. It showed how much the world had changed since I was their age, but I didn't dwell on it. But several days later, when I was talking to a group of salespeople, it occurred to me that there was a broader point.

In any discussion, such as the ones you try to get into every day with clients, prospects, and leads, there's a rhythm to the conversation. It's one that is reflected in the language that's used, the speed at which words are delivered, and the body language of the participants. And it can make a big difference in the outcome of the sale. If you get out of rhythm with that conversation—as I did when I broke in with my stupid question about computer games—you'll disrupt the flow of the discussion and make it that much harder to effectively communicate. Also, if you or someone else sets a bad rhythm to the sales discussion, the sale will probably not happen at all, because there will be no energy involved.

INJECTING ENERGY INTO A PITCH

Let me give you an example.

I once watched a guy selling to a couple of executives. The sale came at the end of a long, hard day. The salesperson had driven to the meeting in a car in which the air conditioning was grumbling and groaning in the middle of a sweltering August day, and I could see (and smell) the sweat that had collected in his armpits and was now running in rivulets down his back. I could tell that all he wanted to do was go back to the office, file his report, go home, and pour himself into a cool martini. Truth to tell, I was in a bit of that sort of mood myself.

As I watched the conversation develop before me, I was struck by two things.

First, there was a lack of energy and drive about it. The salesperson was technically doing everything right: asking questions, letting the executives do most of the talking, trying to find out what they needed rather than offering them solutions to problems they didn't have. But from the outset, his tone was monotonous, his delivery was slow, and he slumped in his chair, barely moving as he spoke.

The second point was that his pitch had degenerated into the kind of jargon that is found in the worst company brochures and sales material. There was nothing fresh or spontaneous about the language he used, and it clearly wasn't connecting with his audience. I was in no way surprised when, at the end of the pitch, the lead executive smiled and said, "Well, I appreciate your time, but I'm afraid this isn't for us."

There are several things to be learned from this kind of experience:

1. **The person setting the tone for the sales discussion drives the sale.** Clearly, you want that person to be you. Getting

there can be challenging if you're up against a strong, assertive personality (although I'm going to show you some tricks in a few minutes to turn that kind of situation around), but it's absolutely essential if you want to win the sale.

2. **No matter how down and tired you're feeling, when you start a sale you've got to summon all the positive energy you can muster.** A lack of energy will *always* translate into your performance.

I've said on several other occasions that selling is a bit like acting. Before actors go out on the stage, they go through energy-building exercises. Sometimes they run around a room, shouting. Sometimes they all hold hands and pass a hand squeeze around the circle as fast as possible. It may sound silly, but believe me, it works. And when they go on stage, that energy communicates to their audience through their performance. You need to find an effective way of doing the same thing before you start to sell.

How can you do it?

Salespeople usually don't sell in teams. So unless there's an unusual set of circumstances, you're not going to have someone else to help you build positive energy. But there are some things you can and should do:

1. **Before going into the sale, get a little exercise.** Try to arrive early and walk up and down the street outside for a minute or two before going in to the meeting. Exercise increases your adrenaline and will give you energy.

2. **If at all possible, start a regular program of exercise.** On your way home from the office, go to the gym for a half hour. Doctors say that ideally you should exercise thirty minutes a day for three to four days a week. That's not a big investment of time, and it can make a crucial difference in the kind of energy you bring to your work.

3. **If you haven't had much (or anything) to eat before going into your sale, bring along a snack**—a chocolate bar, a piece of fruit. Chocolate can give you energy fast; that's why mountain climbers take it in their backpacks.

4. **Above all, remember *why* you want to make this sale.** It's not just that you need the commission, though that's probably a significant motivation. It's that you're helping your client solve a problem. And that's a good thing.

Now that you've built the necessary energy, it's time to set the pace for the conversation. There are several things that will affect this:

- **The speed at which you speak.** If you talk fast, your client will tend to talk fast—we have a strong, natural tendency to imitate the person to whom we're speaking.

- **The words you use.** If you use strong, active words, you'll convey strength and power. Longer words and convoluted sentence structure can bore your audience and confuse them.

- **Your body language.** Using sharp, strong, controlled gestures indicates that you've got clearly thought-out points that you want to convey. On the other hand, if you ramble around the stage when you're speaking or slump in your chair and don't meet your client's eye, chances are you'll come off as confused, insincere, or both.

This is all well and good if you can immediately gain the upper hand in the conversation. But what should you do if the client tries himself to seize the initiative and control the pace and flow of the discussion? This outcome is more common than you might think, because your client is probably just as aware as you are that whoever sets the pace for the discussion holds the advantage.

First of all, don't argue or try to overpower the client by raising your voice or speeding up the discussion. Doing so just results in a very few minutes in people yelling at each other. Instead, you can elect to deliberately break the pattern. If your client starts speaking very rapidly and forcefully in an attempt to dominate things, *slow down*. Take your time answering and asking questions. Place a stress on your thoughtful, reasonable nature.

This strategy works best—and believe me, it's very effective—when you do it by encouraging the client to talk. It may seem counterintuitive; after all, how can you regain control of the conversation if you're doing less talking? But, in fact, the more the client talks, the more he reveals about himself, his company, and the problem he's hoping your product or service will solve. Once you bring that out through artful, open-ended questioning, you can regain the pace and tone of the discussion when you begin to explain the benefits he'll reap from what you're selling. That's just where you want things to be.

READ YOUR AUDIENCE

A key point in all of this is that in a sales pitch, "pace" does not mean "speed." Talking quickly conveys a sense of urgency. Sometimes that's what you want to do. You can persuade your audience that you've got the solution to their pressing problem and you recognize that time is a significant factor in their concerns. That's all well and good. Talking quickly, however, can also give the impression that you're trying to put something over on someone; you're trying to slip in something unsavory.

Part of the trick here is to read your audience and figure out what *they're* comfortable with. Use the conversation before you get into the meat of the sales pitch to find out something about their conversational style. Do they like to speak fast or slow? Do they like a lot of facts or focus more on generalities and vision? Do they enjoy hearing facts and figures, or are they more interested in the "story" part of your pitch?

All these things will go into the crafting of your pitch and the way in which it's delivered. And, as I hope you realize now, the method of delivery can be just as important as the content.

LISTEN BEFORE YOU TALK

16

In the four decades that I've been in sales (has it *really* been that long?) I've evolved a set of rules. This isn't because I'm especially brilliant or intuitive. In fact, for the first several years I was selling, I did things that, looking back on them now, make me shudder.

In particular, I remember going into a presentation to a new client. She was an older woman—well, I was younger then, so she seemed older to me—and with the arrogance of youth, I suspected that she was a bit out of touch with how things worked in the industry.

I'd filled my briefcase with materials, and I was very proud of them. I'd spent hours preparing them, researching the company and studying exactly what it did. I knew its latest stock price performance, its major suppliers, and its organizational structure. I had a list of its top officers committed to memory, as well as the latest facts and figures on its recent merger with a larger company.

In short, I was fully prepared. Or so I thought, anyway. I was so eager to start that I was practically bouncing. In the previous chapter I spoke about the importance of positive energy; well, in this case, I was full of positive energy. I had positive energy coming out of every pore of my body. I could have sold myself anything.

Unfortunately, I forgot an essential rule of selling: I wasn't there to sell things to me; I was there to sell something to the client. That's a distinction that too many salespeople miss, and, as so often happens, it turned the presentation into a disaster.

Not that I had any hint of this problem initially. I sailed into my pitch, facts flying, making jokes along the way. Halfway through, I noticed that the VP wasn't smiling any more. My pleasantries were falling completely flat.

I couldn't figure out what was going on. Surely I hadn't misstated something or involuntarily insulted her by skipping over an important piece of information. Frantic now, my mind scurried back through the past ten minutes, scrambling to find something, anything, I'd done wrong.

I came up empty. I soldiered on, running through my slides. (Back then, we didn't have PowerPoint available to us. My slides were just that—slides in a slide projector.) Finally I came to the end and waited for her response.

She sat quietly for a few minutes and then said in a pleasant tone of voice with a hint of steel running through it, "Steve, how much do you know about our company?"

I was flabbergasted. That was just what my presentation had been *about*! I'd just been *talking* about that! Hadn't she been *listening*?

I swallowed a considerable degree of irritation and said, "I think I know quite a lot. Is there something I've left out?"

She leaned forward a bit. "Do you know anything about how decisions are made here?" she asked.

My stomach doing slow somersaults, I shook my head.

"Do you understand the relationship between management and employees at this company?"

"Uh . . ."

Her voice remained gentle, like a nun chiding an errant child at Catholic school. "I'm not surprised you don't know about those things, Steve. They're not in books or articles. But you could have found out if you'd asked me."

I shook my head, puzzled. "I'm sorry. I don't see what you're getting at here."

"It's very simple." She smiled. "You obviously did a lot of research about us and studied our annual report carefully. You have a very polished presentation, but there are lots of things that go into a decision to buy what you're selling. Some of those you can't find in the materials the company makes available to the public."

I had a feeling, somehow, that I was learning something of great importance here. "So how do I find them out?" I said.

And then she said something that changed my whole philosophy of selling and gave me one of the keys to successful presentations.

"*You've got to ask.*"

START WITH A QUESTION

Elsewhere I've explained the 80/20 rule. It's pretty simple. During a presentation, the salesperson (you) should do about 20 percent of the talking. The client should do the other 80 percent. This isn't just to give the client confidence, although that can be a useful side benefit with some clients. It's that you need, above all, to find out more about whom you're selling to.

That's why I strongly recommend that you start your presentation by asking a question. And then *listen* to the answer.

The ability to actively listen is something that separates good salespeople from bad ones. Active listening includes the following:

- **Focus on the person talking.** If part of your brain is planning the next part of your day or meditating on what you're going to have for lunch, you're not going to

absorb what's being said to you, and you're wasting everyone's time.

- **Acknowledge what's being said.** You can do some of
  this with body language, giving small nods of the head or
  subdued hand gestures to show you've gotten the point
  being made.

- **When you're commenting on what the client has said,
  paraphrase his point before you talk about it.** For
  instance:

Client: You can see that it's extremely important for us to
  have the shipment of widgets delivered at least three
  weeks before the start of the holiday season, so we've got
  time to warehouse and inventory them and get them into
  our system.

Salesperson: I understand. You want to make sure everything's all labeled and numbered and entered into the
  computer in plenty of time for the holidays. Here's what
  we can do to accommodate that . . .

Notice that you don't have to *repeat* exactly what the client said. Sometimes you can do that, but if you do it too much
you'll sound as if you're mocking him, and the sale will go south
very quickly. But paraphrasing summarizes the conversation up
to that point, and it can also help clear up any misunderstandings
or miscommunication.

Ask open-ended questions to follow up. Again, paraphrasing
can be a useful technique here, but use it to keep the conversation
going. Avoid closed questions, to which there's a simple yes or
no answer, because this tends to shut things down. For instance:

Client: The widgets that your company produces seem especially appealing for a younger demographic.

Salesperson: Is your company trying to appeal to eight- to ten-year-olds?

Client: Yes.

Notice that there's an implied pause after the client says, "Yes," because now you've got to get the conversation going again. But if, instead, you direct the conversation this way:

Client: The widgets that your company produces seem especially appealing for a younger demographic-.

Salesperson: That's interesting that you'd say that. Can you tell me something about what customer demographic would be ideal for you?

Client: Well, right now we're starting to shift from exclusively adult items to ones that would attract an audience of teenagers or even a younger group—say, nine- to twelve-year-olds.

Salesperson: I think you'll find that our widgets could effectively serve all three elements of this customer base. So let's discuss how we can do that.

The client, in this exchange, has given you valuable clues as to what he's looking for in your product and how you might be able to help him. Of course, some questions you ask will have a "yes" or "no" answer; sometimes these sorts of questions are unavoidable. But in general it's better to ask open questions, which keep the burden of the conversation on the client. And that's where it should be.

THAT OPENING QUESTION

There's no magic formula about what to ask. In truth, if you've done your research as well as I'd done for that long-ago presentation, you should have a whole list of questions stored up. But the important thing is to get the client talking and to make clear that you're there to learn from her. You want to find out what the problem is so you can help solve it.

Some possible opening questions include:

"Can you tell me something about your company culture?"

"What kind of shifting patterns have you seen in your sales over the past year?"

"Could you tell me who you see as your primary customer?"

"What do you think the primary challenges facing our industry are?"

All of these are general enough to kickstart the conversation.

But Steve, I hear you saying, how do I get from there to the meat of my presentation? The answer is that the presentation, if it's a good one, will flow naturally from the information that you reap from the client. Remember, you don't want to talk *at* the client; you want to talk *to* the client. That's the difference between giving a speech and communicating. (Incidentally, I wish more politicians realized the truth of this concept. Politics in this country would be a lot better if our representatives stopped giving speeches at one another and started to communicate. But that's a subject for another book.)

SCENARIO

It's important as well during the presentation to weave in the information the client has given you and to make sure that you continue to push a back-and-forth dialogue. Consider this:

Salesperson: As you can see on this next slide, during the past two years we've lowered production time on our Primary Widget W-2J from four months to three. We've also improved our quality response time by 18 percent.

It seems to me that this speaks very well to the point you raised earlier about your quality control concerns.

Client: Yes, I agree. You seem to be grappling with this issue.

Salesperson: Perhaps you could explain what particular aspects of quality control are most important to you.

Client: Sure. The most important thing is . . .

And now the client is talking again, and you're listening. Which is the way it should be.

DON'T BE AFRAID OF "I DON'T KNOW"

If you follow the 80/20 rule, chances are overwhelming that the client is going to ask you some questions to which you don't know the answer (as a matter of fact, that's going to happen even if you do most of the talking).

Too many salespeople have convinced themselves that saying, "I don't know the answer to that question" is a sign of unforgivable weakness. I've watched a number of painful moments in which salespeople wiggled and wriggled like a worm on a fishing hook, trying to cover up their lack of knowledge and fake their way through an answer.

Never, never, *never* do that. I've never met a client yet who couldn't see through it. If you make up information on the spot, one of two things will inevitably happen:

1. You'll commit yourself to an obligation that you won't be able to meet.

2. Your misinformation will be discovered, and you'll lose any trust you've built with the client.

Rather than either of these disastrous alternatives, the simplest and best approach is to say, "I don't know the answer to that question. Can I get back to you?" Make a specific commitment, if possible, to a time frame: "I should have an answer for you by next Tuesday, when I've had a chance to talk to my boss." Clients respect a lack of information. But they won't forgive dishonesty—and they shouldn't.

HOW TO ASK
QUESTIONS

like eating out sometimes. I like discovering new restaurants, finding new chefs who want to explore the edges of the culinary experience. Fortunately, I live in New York City, a Mecca for food lovers and restaurant fans. So I can indulge myself in this regard whenever I feel like it. There's always somewhere new to discover.

Sometimes, though, the experience is less than pleasant. Several months ago, I stepped into a new restaurant (new for me, anyway). It was an Italian place, with pleasant decor and Italian-sounding muzak playing quietly in the background. There weren't many people there, and I was looking forward to a nice meal.

The waitress appeared at my elbow. "How are you tonight?" she asked.

I opened my mouth to answer, but she was off. "Welcometo LuigismynameisKathyI'llbetakingcareofyoutonight!" she jerked out in a single breath. "WhatcanIgetforyou?"

I studied the menu, hoping that her speech would get a bit more intelligible as we went on. "How's the linguini with meat-balls?" I asked.

"Linguini with meatballs. Great. You want salad with that?" She was jotting things down busily on her pad.

"No, no. I just want to know how it is?"

She glared at me. "How it *is*?"

"Uh, yes."

She shrugged. "S'great. Is that what you want?"

"Okay, sure." I considered the menu again. "And a glass of Chianti. What's the house wine?"

She stared at the menu as if it was something she'd never seen before. "You want salad with that?"

I didn't bother repeating my question about the wine and simply nodded.

The food, when it came, was actually pretty good. But I never went back to that restaurant, and if anyone asked me about it, I recommended they stay away. And for good reason.

ASKING QUESTIONS MEANS LISTENING

As I said in the previous chapter, you've got to know when to talk and when to listen. The server I encountered at Luigi's (I should say here that this isn't the real name of the restaurant; all names have been changed to protect the innocent) somehow got confused about the purpose of asking questions. That purpose is to *get information*. And that means you've got to know how to listen to the answer and link your next question to it.

The second problem that was illustrated in my exchange with Kathy the Waitress is something I've encountered in salespeople before: They assume they know the answer to a question before they've heard it. Kathy assumed that I wanted the linguini even before I had a chance to make up my mind. It's not uncommon for salespeople to either assume they know what the client wants or to frame their questions in such a way that they force a particular answer.

For example:

Client: Could we talk about order quantity?

Salesperson: Certainly. Since our minimum order is 3,500 units, how much above that would your monthly order be?

Client: Well, as a matter of fact, I wanted to know about placing an order for less than the minimum.

Salesperson: We could consider a discount on anything that's 5,000 units and above. How much of a discount on an order of that size would you be looking for?

Like Kathy and me in the restaurant, the salesperson and the client in this scenario are talking completely past one another. The salesperson has assumed that the client will be ordering more than the minimum and is framing his questions in such a way as to get an answer to a question that the client isn't considering. It's clear that the salesperson isn't hearing what the client's saying— that he wants to place a smaller order—but rather what he wants to hear: a larger order and, consequently, a bigger commission.

It's a shame because in this scenario the salesperson could easily find an opening to push the discussion in other directions. For instance:

Salesperson: Well, an order below the minimum would mean we'd incur some extra production costs, so we'd have to increase the per-unit price. But what would you say to placing a larger order and letting us warehouse half of it for a month until you're ready to distribute the units? There'd be a warehousing fee, but it would probably be cheaper than increasing the per-unit price on a smaller order.

This kind of response reacts to what the client's really concerned with: getting the right number of units for his needs.

Lawyers are generally taught that you should never ask a witness a question to which you don't know the answer. This is a good technique for attorneys trying cases, but it can be very bad for salespeople. Your whole object in the first part of a sales call is to find out as much information as you can. And to do that, you've got to ask a lot of questions to which you *don't* know the answer. You've got to ask them in as open a way as possible; remember that in the previous chapter I stressed the importance of asking open rather than closed questions.

ASKING QUESTIONS MEANS BUILDING ON OTHER QUESTIONS

One excellent technique in asking questions during a sales call is called "layering." The advantage of layering is that it keeps the ball firmly in the client's court as far as talking goes. It's also not at all intimidating. Every now and then you'll hit a client who doesn't like to talk or at least doesn't really like to answer questions. That can be a challenge, and layering is one way to approach it.

A layered question is one that has a number of different levels. You start with a very basic question:

"What's the state of the industry right now?"

After the client has responded, you continue, saying, "That's very interesting. Given this state of affairs, how do you see your company fitting in with the trends?"

And then:

"Since that's your company's strategy, what would you say are your three or four big goalposts over the next twelve months?"

Each layer of the question takes the discussion to a new level. Of course, really, this is one big question about the company's role in the industry, and it offers you plenty of opportunities to explain how your product or service will help the company meet its goals and expand its place in the world.

In general, your questions should always build on the answers to other questions. Doing so keeps the discussion moving forward and gets to more specific issues that you can address. It's also helpful because it shows you've been listening to the client's answers and aren't simply going through a pre-determined script. Harking back to my encounter with Kathy the Waitress, you can see that her opening question wasn't really much of a question. She just had been trained to say that as her first line when approaching a customer. I could have said anything, and it wouldn't have changed the script. That's something to avoid at all costs. Never, *ever* sound rehearsed or artificial. Insincerity is a sale killer.

HELPING THE CLIENT TALK

As I said above, sometimes you run into people who don't like to answer questions. They act as though you're invading their privacy, asking them about some deep, dark secret they've kept hidden away in a locked trunk for years. I met one of them a couple of years ago on a sales pitch to a company I'd done business with for some time. He was new to the staff, and the boss had asked him to talk with me about setting up a training session for the sales department.

I could sense something was wrong from the moment we shook hands. I recommend that salespeople have a strong, firm, confident handshake. It doesn't need to last more than a second or two, but it should convey energy and enthusiasm.

Shaking hands with this guy was like grasping the limp tentacle of a dead squid. His hand was cold, damp, and lifeless. And that was the way he looked as well. Throughout our session I kept feeling that what this guy really needed was a couple of weeks away from work in a sunny place that would get some color and energy back into his body.

I started the way I usually do: asking questions. Quickly it became obvious that this was going to be a struggle. To every question, even the most open-ended ones, he replied in single sentences, sometimes in single words or monosyllabic grunts. I could feel the energy draining out of the room in barrelfuls.

I decided to try something radical. After he gave a single-sentence answer to one of my questions, rather than going on with my pitch I sat and looked at him in silence. Moments passed and he began to look a bit annoyed. Finally he said, "Aren't you going to go on?"

"I can," I told him, "but I think it would be more useful if you would expand on what you just said."

He thought for a moment, then said a bit more. Again, I sat and looked at him. And finally, he continued, adding something else to his previous explanation.

I won't say that he became talkative after that. But at least he began to give me a bit more to work with, and I wound up setting up a good deal. The lesson I took away is this: Silence is a vacuum, and people feel compelled to fill it. So if you want to get a client to talk, resist the temptation to fill the silences yourself and let him do it for you. Once you get him talking, your main problem may be to get him to be quiet. But that's a good problem to have.

I've spent a lot of time on questions because they're an essential part of what we as salespeople do. One of the first skills a salesperson should learn is the art of asking questions. So here are the main points you should take away from the last couple of chapters:

1. **Ask questions throughout your presentation.** That's the only way you'll get the information you need to make the sale.

2. **You should do about 20 percent of the talking during the presentation.** The client should do the other 80 percent.

3. **Ask open questions rather than closed ones.** An open question is one that requires something more than a "yes" or "no" answer. The object is to get the client talking.

4. **Ask questions that build on others.** Layered questions are a helpful way of doing this.

5. **Never sound rehearsed or scripted.** If you catch yourself doing this, find a way to break up your presentation. It should be a dialogue, not a speech.

6. **Don't feel compelled to fill silences with talk.** Sometimes it's better just to wait for the client to start talking.

TEN THINGS YOU SHOULD *NEVER* SAY

18

Positive selling techniques are all about attitude, confidence, and a belief in yourself and what you're selling. I firmly believe that if you follow the advice in this book—advice that's been honed over more years of experience than I care to remember—your sales will increase, sometimes dramatically. At the same time, I want to caution you: There's no magic formula that's always going to get you the sale. Sometimes a sale just won't happen, no matter what you do. In these cases, you need to know when, just as in a poker game, it's best to get up from the table and cash in your chips.

However, the best thing that you can do as a positive salesperson is create the best possible conditions in which a sale is most likely to happen. That said, there are certain things you can do that will all but guarantee that the sale will fail. These things put needless obstacles in your way, sour the conversation, and create unneeded tension.

And at one point or another in my career, I've said all of them.

I'd like to think that after reading this chapter you'll never again make the same mistake. But I'll settle for you being aware of the damage they can do to a sales conversation and trying, as much as you, can to avoid them.

1. **You don't really want that.**

    When you walk into a sales call, you should know the product or service better than anyone in the room. You should also know a lot about what your client's needs and wants are and how what you're selling will solve the problem. So there's a natural tendency, when someone starts going off on a particular feature she or he wants, or an aspect of delivery or pricing she or he feels is necessary, that you *know* won't work . . . there's just a normal desire on your part to say, "You don't really want that."

    Refrain from that desire.

    Personally, I can tell you that nothing sets my teeth more on edge than someone telling me what's good for me or bad for me. The older I get, the more people try to tell me such things, and the more it ticks me off. I want to shout at them, "Dammit, I'm an adult! I can make decisions! And *I'll* decide what I do and don't want. If I make a mistake, I'll take responsibility for it, but don't *ever* try to take away my ability to choose."

    Because I know how I react, I know how clients tend to react when you say this to them. It's not that all their decisions are good or rational; quite often they're not. But while you can gently warn them of the consequences of what they're proposing, don't take away their right to make mistakes.

2. **My company will never do that.**

    "Never," like all absolutes, is a very big word. Never is a long time, and in this fast-paced world things can change on a dime. If the client asks you to do something, your first reaction should always be to think about ways you *could* be accommodating—even if it means breaking new ground. You don't have to commit to anything unreasonable, and you shouldn't. But at worst you can say, "Well, that would be a big step for us, because we haven't done anything like it before. Let me talk it over with my boss and get back to you on it." Such a response marks you as reasonable, open to change, aware of the consequence of what the client is proposing, and concerned with not violating the chain of command at your company. Those are all qualities the client will respect because they're the kinds of things she or he looks for in her or his own employees.

3. **There's nothing to discuss.**

Wrong, wrong, wrong! There's *always* something to discuss. This kind of statement is the moral equivalent of getting up and marching out of the room, slamming the door behind you. It's pointlessly aggressive and shuts down the whole conversation. The client's reaction, a perfectly reasonable one, is going to be, "If there's nothing to discuss, why are we talking?" And before you know it, you're out the door, in your car, and heading back to the office, hoping like anything that you get a chance to explain to your boss what happened before the client calls him.

Never close the door to discussion. Even if the client closes it for you, do your best to pry the door back open a crack. If the discussion gets hostile, find a way to cool it down. Change the subject, propose a break, or ask for a glass of water. Anything to give everyone a chance to go to their respective corners and think about things.

4. **You don't need to know.**

This might be perfectly true. There are all sorts of things the client doesn't need to know. But she's the one who's going to make that decision, not you. Of course, that doesn't mean you need to give her proprietary information if she asks—though there are polite ways of explaining to her that you really can't discuss your sales figures for the quarter or tell her the size of the deal you just did with the firm across town. But there's no need to be confrontational. Just smile and say something like, "Well, I'm afraid that information is confidential, but rest assured we extend that same confidentiality to all of our clients, including you. So you and I can maintain trust between us because I can assure you I'll never share the contents of our negotiations with anyone outside my company."

5. **Nobody else needs to know about this.**

I've heard this phrase come out of the mouths of salespeople, and I'm always stunned when they say it. I can't think of another sentence more calculated to destroy a client's trust.

Clients aren't stupid. They know perfectly well that you're going to have to report the details of your deal to your superiors, and it's going to have to be approved up the line, probably with sign offs from various executives. So telling them that somehow you can do a deal that will be under the table, even a little, means to them that you're not loyal to your organization. And if you can't be loyal to your own company, how on earth can you be loyal to them?

This kind of suggestion marks you as sleazy, possibly even criminal. No matter how sweet the deal you're offering, no reasonable client will touch it after that. You'll be surprised how quickly word gets around that you're not to be trusted.

As a salesperson, at the end of the day, what you have is your integrity. Never give that away.

6. **The details don't matter.**

Yes, they do! The devil, as someone famously said, is in the details. The details of a deal are where the nitty-gritty matters of dollars and cents get hammered out. Elsewhere I've strongly recommended that, whenever possible, you be the one to draw up the final version of a contract. That's because it's precisely in the language of the contract that the significant terms of the deal will be defined.

If you're just a "big picture" person with contempt for or lack of interest in details, you may close a lot of sales, but I guarantee you won't make much money and you won't stay in any job long. Train yourself to focus on details and nail them down during the sale.

That said, sometimes you get to a point where both of you are exhausted and it's better and easier to say something like, "I think we can work out these details through e-mail. I'll draft a contract and then we'll discuss the exact wording."

7. **You'll have to live with it.**

No client wants to hear from you that you're not willing to make an effort on his behalf. This is true even if you know that the effort is pointless. When a client says, "I need delivery of that stock the day after Christmas," he doesn't want to hear you saying that there's no point in even discussing this because your warehouse isn't open then.

It's much better to say, "Well, that's a problem for us, but let me get back to you after talking to my supervisor."

If the answer from the supervisor is "no," at least you're not the one wearing the black hat. Besides, you never can tell. Sometimes the answer will be "yes."

8. **We're never going to agree.**

This is an atom bomb of a statement—guaranteed to leave a sales discussion a smoking ruin. I've had clients throw it at me every now and again, mostly as a negotiating tactic. Sometimes, of course, when a sale is going badly, it's tempting to hurl this into the mix and get out of the room before you empty the water pitcher over someone. I know just how that feels, and I sympathize. Nonetheless, I warn you against saying this, because it dooms the possibility of a sale.

Even when you seem miles apart, there are ways of finding your way around just about any objection (see my book *The 25 Toughest Sales Objections* for strategies on how to do this). As I said earlier, "never" is a big word, and it's rarely accurate. Given enough time and patience, you can get agreement—and the sale.

9. **That's never going to happen.**

Here we go with "never" again. I'd advise you to expunge that word from your vocabulary. You can use words such as "unlikely," "improbable," "unusual," and "challenging." But "never"? No.

Times change. Things that I thought I'd never see are commonplace today. When I was growing up, computers were giant machines that ran on miles of electronic tape. Phones were big, black, and you could knock someone over with the receiver. Televisions were massive and they sat in huge cabinets, while the family gathered around them to watch the Sunday afternoon football game.

So "never"? I don't think so.

When the client puts up a seemingly impossible request, try to modify his expectations and then, without committing absolutely to anything, try to find something to give him. If you can't, at least you tried.

10. **I can absolutely guarantee that.**

I can hear you say, "Why wouldn't you say that? That's what a client wants to hear."

Of course they do. But the problem is the word, "absolutely." It's another one of those words that impose an unreasonable set of expectations on any deal. After all, you can only guarantee things up to a point. Anything could happen. Earthquakes, storms, Martian invasions. Your warehouse could burn down tomorrow, and there'd be nothing you could do to make the agreed-upon deal happen.

A guarantee can be a very powerful sales tool, but it should be used carefully. Don't accompany it with "absolutely," because I guarantee if you do, sooner or later you'll be sorry. And that's about as absolute a guarantee as I can give.

ENDING THE FIRST CONVERSATION

19

A friend of mine—I'll call her Mary—told me about a sales experience she had several years ago. She was meeting with a prospect, someone who'd expressed an interest in buying from her company but hadn't committed to anything. It took several weeks to get a meeting with him, but at last she succeeded.

"I can give you twenty minutes," he told her. "Let's meet at 10 AM I can free some time up then."

She arrived on time (slightly ahead of schedule, actually) and was ushered into his office. She made her pitch, duly asking him questions, determining his needs, and so on.

She was very absorbed in the conversation and felt it was going extremely well. She was confident that her product met exactly the challenges in his business that he described to her, and she could tell from his tone and body language that he was impressed. She pressed on, looking for the clear signs of commitment: the indication that he was willing to sign on to a deal.

The executive had a couple of paper clips in front of him, and she noticed as they talked that he began to push them around. Then he un-bent them and folded them around one another. They grew tighter and tighter, and although his voice was polite, she could feel tension building.

"How about if we just wrap things up?" she suggested. "I think we've come to an agreement, and I'll draw up the paperwork when I get back to my office."

To her surprise, he shoved back his chair abruptly and stood up. "I don't think so!" he said. "I'm sorry to have wasted your time, but we're not interested. Now, if you'll excuse me, I have another appointment."

And that was that.

Mary and I discussed this over a drink, and she wanted my opinion. What had gone wrong?

KNOW WHEN TO PUSH— AND WHEN NOT TO

For some reason, the whole thing made me feel like Sam Spade from Dashiell Hammet's classic noir novel *The Maltese Falcon*. I could almost feel the San Francisco fog rolling in. (The fact that the bar where we were having the drink was in Lower Manhattan didn't seem to make much difference.) If I'd had a fedora, I would have pulled it a little lower over my eyes and flipped up the collar of my trench coat.

I had a couple of clues from what she'd told me:

1. The guy was a new prospect, and this was the first time she'd met with him about her company and her line of products.

2. He was clearly busy.

3. He'd cleared twenty minutes in the middle of the morning, when things are usually especially hectic.

4. He'd become increasingly tense as the meeting went on.

5. He ended things very abruptly and on a harsh, negative note.

I asked Mary a couple of questions, which she answered readily.

Yes, she'd pushed hard for the sale. Her company was struggling to make its numbers for the quarter, and she knew that it had only a couple of weeks to do so. Yes, she'd listened to his concerns about the product and addressed them. No, she didn't know off-hand how long they'd been talking, though it didn't seem that long. And yes, as the meeting went on, he spoke less and less, and she spoke more and more. She knew he was becoming less responsive to her pitch, but she couldn't think of anything to do except keep talking.

DON'T ASK FOR TOO MUCH

In Hammet's novel, Caspar Guttman, the villainous fat man, chuckles when talking to Sam Spade. "By Gad, sir!" he declares. "You're a character!"

I waited for a moment to see if Mary was going to say anything like that to me. She didn't, so I told her what I thought. Here it is in a nutshell.

She pushed so hard that despite her best intentions, she broke the sale. She forgot one of the basic rules of selling: You can only sell as much as the other party wants to buy.

Selling—*good* selling—is not about getting people to buy things they don't need. That sort of thing, if it belongs anywhere, should be confined to late-night television infomercials, broadcast when right-thinking people are sound asleep. But good selling is about making win-win deals with clients, deals that benefit them by solving a problem for them. You can't rush that.

It's notable that the prospect in Mary's case was willing to meet with her and, moreover, to meet with her right at a point when he'd normally be busy with a lot of important things. So clearly he assigned a great deal of importance to Mary's visit. She should have recognized that right away and realized that she should adhere *strictly* to the rules he'd set up, the main one being that he only had twenty minutes to talk to her.

Rather than use that twenty minutes most productively, as a springboard for a follow up meeting, she pushed hard for a commitment. He didn't want to make it without further thought, possibly so he could consult with other people on his staff. In any case, as soon as she ran into that wall—detectable by his growing silence and his twisting of paperclips—Mary should have smiled, stood, and brought the meeting to an end. By doing that, she'd have shown that she respected his time and appreciated that he gave her twenty minutes of it.

Sometimes people think that positive selling means you've got to push, that being positive means never stepping back from something. That's not really the point. Positive selling also means knowing what you can and should get from any given meeting. In this case, Mary needed to see the sale as a multi-step process, one that would require several additional meetings and some patience on her part. Yes, she was feeling pressured by the front office to make the sale, but as a result of pushing, she got nothing—just a prospect that went "poof!" and was gone with the wind.

HOW TO END A MEETING

At the end of any meeting—particularly one such as the one Mary was involved in—there is a series of specific steps you should take:

1. **End on a good note.** Even if you and the other party have been at loggerheads the whole time, find something positive and cheerful to say to close things out. You want to leave everyone with a happy memory of the discussion so they'll be willing to come back for more.

2. **Summarize what was discussed.** This doesn't have to be a long-winded speech—after all, you're trying to end the

meeting, not continue it. But it's important that everyone agree on the points that were covered.

3. **Outline the main points of agreement.** Again, this doesn't have to be long, and in a short meeting such as the one Mary was describing to me, it probably wasn't. Twenty minutes isn't a lot of time to agree on a wide range of issues. But here, in particular, it's essential that everyone know where the next meeting will start

4. **Set a time and place for the next meeting.** This is probably the most important thing you can do, and if you get nothing else out of the meeting, get this. Even if the whole first meeting is spent on superficialities, as long as you've got a time and place to talk again, you've made progress. Sometimes an initial meeting isn't about much of anything except getting to know one another. That's fine! Just be sure you don't leave it at that.

The problem Mary had was that the prospect had cut off any chance of another meeting. The only thing she could do, I told her, was screw up her courage, make the phone call, apologize, and try to retrieve something from the wreckage.

That's important too, by the way. Just because a meeting ends with someone slamming the door, you don't have to give up. Sometimes the catharsis of door-slamming helps clear the air a bit. I don't especially recommend it as a sales technique, but don't take it as the end of everything either.

All in all, ending a meeting is about meeting the client's needs. You have to read his body language to know when continuing will be counterproductive. The twisted paperclips should have been a big alarm bell for Mary. Likewise, the silence of the prospect should have told her that he was disengaged from the sale and there wasn't any point in continuing. She should have picked up on these things and moved to close the discussion on a strong, positive note.

I suggested all this to Mary, and she frowned, considering it. Then she ordered another drink.

"So what did I get out all that?" she asked. "Maybe another chance, if I'm lucky. Most likely a failed sale."

I hitched my stool up closer to the bar and told her a bit about the ending of *The Maltese Falcon*. (I'm not giving too much away here, but if you've never read the book: spoiler alert!) It's an oddly nihilistic book in some ways. Justice is done in the end, but not with a lot of happiness. Spade, the protagonist, doesn't get the fabulously valuable falcon statue that's at the heart of the book. Nor does he get the girl. He doesn't even get the money to cover his expenses for the several days the case took. He loses his partner and complicates his already shaky relationship with the San Francisco Police Department.

So what does he get out of it all? Experience, I suppose. Knowing a little more about human nature and how it works. And for a salesperson such as Mary, that's not a bad thing to get from a failed sale either. Because the next time she'll know more about how to close a meeting and get what she wants from it.

I stood up and looked around. The streets outside the bar were slick with rain. Taxi cabs were squawking for passengers. And a little fog was even coming up from the damp pavements in the warm summer evening.

"See you later!" I told her. I turned up the collar of my trench coat and went out into the night.

THE IMPORTANCE OF POSITIVE FOLLOW UP

20

A salesperson I knew spent weeks preparing for an important call. He researched, contacted all the right people throughout the prospective company he was trying to sell to, and made elaborate, color-coded charts showing who reported to whom, so he'd be aware of protocol when talking to everyone there. He rehearsed his presentation several times with his coworkers and once or twice with his wife, apparently. He assembled an impressive set of PowerPoint slides—images, words, and numbers were whizzing in and out with "zips!" "pings!" and "whooshes!"

And the day of the presentation seemed to justify all that preparation. He sailed through it without a hitch. Everyone who heard it agreed it was one of the best and most impressive sales talks they'd ever heard.

Flushed with success, he went back to the office and reported gleefully to his superiors that the whole thing was in the bag. And then . . . nothing. For three days, the head of the company, my friend's boss, waited for word that the deal had gone through, that the contracts were drawn up and awaiting review by the firm's legal team. After three days of deafening silence, he called his salesman into the office.

"What's going on with X Company?" he asked.

"Oh," said the salesman airily, "I'm letting that one mature a bit."

"Have you talked to them since your presentation?"

"No." The salesperson sensed something was wrong with the conversation as it was going and added hastily, "But I will. I just don't want to rush things on a deal this important."

His boss nodded. "All right," he said. "But if I don't hear anything about this by next week, I'm going to be very concerned."

Sure enough, the next week rolled around without a peep out of the salesperson. This time when the boss called him in, he was angry.

"This is a big deal!" he snapped. "What's going on?"

The salesperson looked sheepish. "Well," he said, "I'll call this afternoon and find out what's happening."

There was silence. You could have dropped an iceberg into the room and it wouldn't have made it any colder. Finally, the boss spoke, his voice sounding like a frozen razor blade.

"Do you mean to tell me," he said, "that you haven't spoken to them *at all* since your presentation?"

The salesman didn't have to say anything. He knew he was hip deep in trouble.

OUT OF SIGHT, OUT OF MIND

I'd like to tell you that this story has a happy ending, but you can probably guess it doesn't. The salesman had, on the strength of his presentation, simply sat on the prospect for two weeks without following up. And the result? Just what you'd expect. The company turned around and did a deal with someone else. All that work, all that great presentation for nothing.

When the salesman told me this story some months after it happened, I asked, just as I know you want to, "What happened? Why didn't you call?"

He shrugged wearily. "I just thought that they'd follow up," he said. "They obviously wanted the deal. So I wanted to make them come to me and ask for it. I figured that would give me the upper hand in negotiations."

I shook my head sadly. It's one of Schiffman's Commandments: Thou shalt not make the customer take the initiative. And I could see here the consequences of disobeying it.

The fact of the matter is, no matter how good your presentation, no matter how strong your grasp of the facts, when you walk out that door after a sales call, you go right out of everyone's mind. That's not because they're forgetful or flakey—they've just got a thousand other things to think about. After all, they've got a company to run.

Think of your sales call like a garden. I feel a bit embarrassed, really, using this analogy—when it comes to gardening, I've got something of a black thumb. House plants look at me coming, wither up, and start dropping leaves on the carpet. Any herbs I've tried to grow in pots on the windowsill soon give up the ghost. Nonetheless, I think the example works. When you plant seeds, it's essential that you continue to pay attention to them. If you just stick them in the ground and don't bother to water them or, in the case of house plants, turn them toward the light occasionally, they'll probably die. In the same way, without strong follow up, the points you made in your sales call won't stay alive long enough to germinate and grow into healthy plants. You have to continue to nourish them and cultivate them. And if you do that, they'll bear fruit.

THE ELEMENTS OF FOLLOW UP

In the previous chapter I discussed how to successfully end a conversation, and I stressed the importance of setting up a second meeting. This is the first part of your positive follow up; you need a chance to continue the conversation with the client, to continue exploring his needs so you can explain how your product or service gratifies them. In gardening terms, you need to regularly water your plants.

The second element of follow up is your e-mail or letter. This is something you should send as soon as you get back to the office. Ideally, it should reach your client or prospect within twenty-four hours of your conversation.

The e-mail (I'll assume it's going to be an e-mail because these days hardly anyone sends actual letters anymore) should do the following things:

1. Thank the client for taking the time to meet with you.

2. Remind him or her of the most important things you discussed.

3. Reiterate the agreed-upon time and place of your next meeting.

4. Highlight a couple of things about what you're selling. If possible, these should be things you didn't mention during the sales call, things that will be news to the recipient.

5. Mention anyone else you were introduced to during the sales call.

6. Thank the client again for his or her time and interest.

The note doesn't have to be long; in fact, it shouldn't be—writing three or four paragraphs is just fine. But what it does is keep you and what you're selling in front of the client's eyes.

The third element of positive follow up comes up a couple of days later. You should spend part of that time looking for information that will be useful or interesting to the client—something from the Internet or a newspaper or another news source. Send the prospect a second note with a link to the information. This note can be very short, something along the lines of "Just thought in view of our conversation the other day you might find this interesting, especially given the light it sheds regarding . . ."

Whether the client reads the article is irrelevant. This note does two things: First, it keeps you front and center in the client's mind; second, it gives you a jumping off point for your next meeting. You can begin, "Hey, I wonder if you had a chance to look at that link I sent you last week concerning . . ."

Of course, the last thing you want to do is make a pest of yourself. Subconsciously, I think that was the problem that my friend—the one whose story I told at the beginning of this chapter—was wrestling with. He didn't want to seem overly pushy, so he chose to step back and wait for the client to make the first move.

But I've got news. The client will *never* make the first move. After all, why should he?

WOOING THE CLIENT

The client, remember, has alternatives. If he doesn't like what you're selling or the way you're selling it, he can go to one of your competitors.

The whole business reminds me of the now-largely-forgotten art of wooing. I realize that I may sound hopelessly old-fashioned here, but hear me out. Back in the day, if you wanted to get a girl to go out with you, you'd call her, ask her on a date, and then, if you were serious and the date went well, you'd ask her out again.

Of course, if the girl was popular there were a half dozen other guys all calling her up as well. And I assure you that any guy who, after a first successful date with a popular girl, sat next to the phone and said, "I'll wait for her to make the first move. I want her to come to me," was in for some long, lonely Friday and Saturday evenings. In fact, the first thing I used to do after a particularly successful date was to call the girl the *minute* I got home and tell her what a great time I had. I was selling myself to her, and I wanted her to know what a great deal she was getting. (My wife has, perhaps understandably, a somewhat different perspective on this, but she can write about that in her own book.)

Another way to look at it is this: All of your follow up, all of the work you put in after that initial sales call is preparation. For what? For the second sales call. Because if you can keep the cycle going, that's the secret to developing a long, successful relationship.

In the previous chapter, I described the consequences of being too pushy. My friend Mary pressed too hard for the resolution of a sale in that first meeting and it backfired on her. In this chapter we're considering the opposite problem—what happens if you don't seem to want the sale enough to follow up. The answer's the same in both cases: You don't get the sale.

The solution lies in the middle. Doing the kind of follow up I've described makes you seem interested and helpful but not desperate or pushy. What you're after is a conversation, one that continues for a long time over many years. It's during that conversation that you'll find out more and more about the client, about how you can help him solve problems. You'll find that the relationship matures and settles down to a rhythm that both of you are comfortable with.

So in that respect, it's exactly like marriage. And that's not a bad thing at all.

PART III
FROM START TO CLOSE

TYPES OF CLIENTS

21

When I was growing up, one of the books I read over and over was *The Adventures of Sherlock Holmes*. Thanks to Arthur Conan Doyle's master detective, I grew up with a vague picture of London as a city of gaslight and swirling fog, where mysterious figures slipped in and out of doorways, followed by a tall, gaunt figure clad in a voluminous cape and deerstalker hat, the stem of a curved pipe gripped between his teeth. During my teenage years and on into adulthood, I gradually read the entire Holmes canon: fifty-six short stories and four novels.

At various times, I've found myself returning to them, not only because I think they're amazingly well written and exciting stories that still have the power to keep me engrossed, but because I find useful lessons in them about people, sales, and life in general.

One of the amusing features of the stories is Holmes's constant ability to astonish his companion, Dr. Watson, with his deductions about people they encounter. In "The Red-Headed League," for example, Holmes's client is a pawnbroker named Jabez Wilson. As he sits in their sitting room at 221B Baker Street, Watson looks Wilson over. Holmes notices him doing so and says, cheerfully, "Beyond the obvious facts that he has at some time done manual labor, that he takes snuff, that he is a Freemason, that he has been in China, and that he has done a considerable amount of writing lately, I can deduce nothing else."

Both Watson and Wilson are astonished until Holmes explains exactly how he came to each of these deductions, after which the whole matter seems ridiculously obvious to both of them.

I bring all this up because one of the things being in sales for thirty years has taught me is an ability to recognize certain types of clients. I don't claim to have a Holmesian faculty of observation, but I can still spot some types immediately when we start talking.

This is useful, because, as I've remarked in some of my other books, you have to attune your pitch to the type of client you're dealing with. This is a case where a one-size-fits-all approach is going to present significant trouble for you if you try it.

At the same time, even though clients can be divided into types, they don't necessarily want to believe that. That font of wisdom Groucho Marx once said, "Everyone thinks he's an individual and everyone else is nothing." Sales illustrates that point extremely well. Everyone you'll ever sell to has a problem, and every one of them will tell you that their problem is unique.

FOUR MAJOR TYPES

In *25 Toughest Sales Objections* I examined each sales objection in light of four different types of clients. It's worth running over this again, because you're going to encounter these types constantly in the field.

Dominant

These people are aggressive, opinionated, and challenging. They won't take anything you say on faith, and they want to see proof in the form of statistics, charts, and graphs for every assertion you make. They push hard in negotiations, and often they'll try to use the force of their personality to intimidate you.

Remember what I said earlier about Attitude? These people have it in spades.

The bad: Dominant personalities can be exhausting to deal with because they make you go over and over the same ground until they're completely satisfied. They can be annoying because they push and push, often beyond any point you'd consider reasonable. And even when a deal is completed and you've all agreed on the terms of the sale, they'll keep pushing about everything, from the timing of the signed contracts to the details of the execution of the deal.

The good: Once you've finally convinced them of your bona fides, dominant personalities can become extremely loyal customers. It takes a lot of effort to reel them in, so they tend to stick to you once you've got them. That's not to say they won't continue to be demanding, but they'll be inclined to stay with you unless you completely screw up.

Influence

These personalities seem, at first glance, to be the complete opposite of dominants. They're all about the warm and fuzzy aspects of a sales relationship. They want to know about you, your family, your friends, and how you spent your summer vacation. They're the ultimate networkers, and often you'll find that they've been in touch in one way or another with half the people in your organization. They've mastered social media—such things as Facebook, LinkedIn, and Twitter—and they use them constantly to maintain their networks.

The bad: Influence people, like dominants, can be very exhausting, but for different reasons. They want you to constantly stay in touch, and they've got a million questions. Many of them are about your product, but a lot of them are about you. If you're the kind of person who resists sharing too much information with comparative strangers, this can be a very uncomfortable type to deal with.

The good: The power of networking is increasing in importance in the world of sales, just as it is everywhere else. Through your contact with influence clients, you can expand your range of prospects and leads and get a better handle on what's happening in the industry. Just remember that influence personalities aren't necessarily discrete with information. They share freely, so whatever you tell them can easily make its way through their entire network.

Steadiness

I have to confess that of the four groups discussed here, this is the one I have the hardest time dealing with. They're nice, yes, almost at the level of influence clients. They're thorough too. Not quite to the degree of dominant clients, but right up there. But because they really, really want to be sure their decision is the right one, they debate about it to distraction. Every time you think you're getting close to getting a firm commitment from them, they back away and want more data.

The bad: Well, obviously, the worst problem is that a steadiness client can talk a sales deal to death. Matters can get so frustrating that you want to just get up and walk out of the room. (Full disclosure: I've done that a couple of times. Not that I'm proud of it.) And everything about the sales process drags on interminably.

The good: Like dominant clients, steadiness clients are firm in their commitments once they've been made. They've spent so much energy and thought getting to the point of a deal that they don't want to go back on it. And if you gain their trust, some of their OCD features ease up a bit with time.

Conscientious

Like dominant or steadiness clients, these people want a lot of data to work from. But unlike either of these groups, they're incapable of expressing enthusiasm. In fact, they tend to play their cards very close to the vest. It's extremely difficult to know what a conscientious client is thinking, and often you have to work very hard to get them to give helpful answers to your questions. They don't feel comfortable with anyone outside their immediate circle—in this respect, they're the mirror opposite of influence personalities. And even when you've completed a deal with them, they're unlikely to let you in.

The bad: Dealing with a conscientious personality can be exhausting, because it's like trying to get a teenager to engage in conversation. It can be done; it just takes a lot of work, and sometimes you wonder at the end if it was worth it. Conscientious types have mastered the art of sitting quietly and letting you do all the work in a sales call. That's not what you want, of course. You want the client talking so you can use the information she gives you. But conscientious clients aren't inclined to give you that information, so you've got to work a lot harder for it.

The good: Conscientious clients operate from logic rather than emotion. They're like Mr. Spock aboard the starship *Enterprise*. They may not get very excited, but their decisions are usually sound because they're based on facts and figures and not their guts. You're going to have to work hard to convince them that your product or service can help them, but lots of data is the key to success with them.

VARIATIONS ON TYPES

As I say, I flatter myself that I can usually tell within a few minutes of talking to a prospect, lead, or client which of these four types she or he fits into. At the same time, I have to stop myself from pigeonholing people. Sometimes, when you think you know someone, the person can surprise you with an unexpected quirk. Even after thirty-five or forty years of close friendship, there were a few occasions when Dr. Watson managed to surprise Sherlock Holmes.

As well, people are individuals, and each one of them has his or her own approach to things. The types that I've listed here are simply a useful guide for you, a way of approaching a sales call and figuring out the best approach to the person or people you're going to be selling to.

In reviewing this chapter, I suggest that as much as possible you focus on the good elements for each type rather than the bad. You can't ignore the negative aspects of each character type, but keep them from crowding out the positives. When you run into a Dominant who's driving you crazy with his questions and constant in-your-face style of discussion, remember that once you've convinced him that you've got what he wants, he'll have your back. When a Steadiness client is making your stomach churn because of her inability to come to a decision, keep in mind that with time, it'll get better. She'll trust you more and not agonize so much over every decision.

MEETING
OBJECTIONS

22

It so happens that I've written an entire book on how to overcome sales objections (*25 Toughest Sales Objections and How to Overcome Them*). So I've given this subject a lot of thought.

I've had to, because in training salespeople, it's one of the questions I come up against the most frequently: What do you do when the customer says no?

I'm not going to repeat the entire book, but I'll make the most basic point to you right up front: A sales objection is nothing but an unrecognized sales opportunity. This idea is at the heart of the philosophy of positive selling.

I'm not just blowing smoke at you either. I firmly believe that there are very few objections that can't be overcome. That isn't to say you'll make the sale every time; sometimes you'll have to put it off or take a while to properly cultivate it. But in most cases, if you handle it the right way, you'll come away with a sealed deal.

THE FIRST STEP

Here are some of the most common objections:

- The price is too high.

- I don't need that.

- I don't like the rep.

- It doesn't do what I need it to do.

- I'm not ready to make a decision.

At some point, you've probably heard all of these objections—sometimes during the same sales call. And when you do hear them, it can feel like walking into a door. You stop and stare at the person who's making the objection. A hundred thoughts flit through your brain, starting with, "You have *got* to be kidding me!" Then you recover and, if you've read my book and absorbed my philosophy, you move on.

The first thing you have to do is determine if the objection is a real objection. It might not be. It might be:

- A negotiating tactic aimed at weakening your position even before you've finished your pitch.

- The result of a misunderstanding—either the client has heard you incorrectly or you haven't said the right things.

- The result of a factor entirely external to you. One particularly obnoxious client hurled objection after objection at me, and I found out later that she was going through a nasty divorce and was intent or destroying any male who crossed her path.

Assuming that the objection is legitimate, you then have to do something that a lot of salespeople seem to find difficult: You have to acknowledge its validity. This is *not* to say that you need to back away with your tail between your legs. You don't have to tell the client that she's right when she tells you what you're selling is entirely wrong for her business. You just have to acknowledge that her concern is genuine. Consider the two conflicting scenarios here:

Client: I'm sorry. I appreciate your time, but I'm afraid the product doesn't perform the way we need it to.

Salesperson: What do you mean?

Client: Well, we need it to process a minimum of fifteen units per minute, and your specs say it only does ten.

Salesperson: Okay, let me explain to me why you're wrong. First, I don't think you really need it to do fifteen units a minute. My research says you could get ten units a minute and—

Client: Okay, we're done here.

Not the way you want to end a sales call. But consider this:

Client: I'm not inclined to make a deal here. What you're selling doesn't meet our needs at this time.

Salesperson: I'm sorry. Could you explain a bit more?

Client: Well, we're moving away from that part of the industry, so it's not necessary for us to be nearly as up to date on the technology. I think we'd just be spending money on a product we wouldn't use that much.

Salesperson: I see. I can certainly understand that you don't want to make expenditures that aren't going to give you a reasonable return on investment. But could you explain to me something more about the direction in which your company is heading.

Client: Absolutely. Be glad to.

Here's the basic difference between the two approaches: The first is confrontational and implicitly demeans the client. No wonder she brought to sales call to a swift end. No one likes to be told she doesn't understand her own needs—even if it's true.

The second approach acknowledges that the client has raised a reasonable point and moves the conversation on from there. Notice that the salesperson doesn't make any snap judgment about whether the target company is making the right decision or not. He just tries to find out more about it and develop an approach that will meet his client's needs.

GETTING PAST THE OBJECTION

Once you've established that the objection is real and not just some tactical move on the part of the client, and you've acknowledged to her that you understand and appreciate the problem she's got, you need to start helping her solve the problem. In other words, you've got to move the conversation away from the objection and toward a solution. By doing so, you change the tone of the exchange from negative to positive. Now you're not concerned anymore with what's wrong; rather, you want to find out what would be right.

It's useful here to ask what qualities the client would look for in a successful product or service from you. This allows you to clearly identify what the client's looking for and determine if there's a reasonable solution. It also keeps the client talking, which is essential at this stage of things. The last thing you want is a conversation partner who tells you he's not going to buy what you're selling and then shuts up like a bad-tempered oyster.

Now that you've established the way in which the client wishes your solution would work, you have to evaluate whether you can, in fact, provide such an answer. If you can, the rest of the call is easy. However, there's a better than 50 percent chance that you can't—after all, if you could, the objection probably wouldn't have arisen in the first place.

This is where you need to negotiate with the client. You start by explaining that you can do what the client wants. In truth, you can almost always do what the client wants—but at a price. That's what you have to communicate. This will precipitate an often lengthy series of back-and-forth exchanges, bargaining over the details. But the important point is that the discussion has moved forward and is on the track not of what you can't do for the client but of what you can do.

Which means you've gotten past the biggest part of the objection.

Of course, there are some objections that simply can't be overcome. If the client says flatly, "I'm not going to buy from you, and you can't make me change my mind," it's not worth fighting. But, as I point out in my book, even in that case it's essential to lay the groundwork for a future relationship and to find a way to follow up later. If you follow this course rather than doing what you're probably tempted to do—stalking out of the meeting and deleting the client's name from your contact list—you'll find more often than not at some point in the future you'll be sitting in the same conference room, talking to the same people, and showing them proudly how their new sets of problems and issues can be solved by your company.

THE ANGRY CLIENT

23

As I've made clear in this and other books, when my temper is stirred it tends to be a maelstrom.

It's not that I'm a naturally angry person—I'm not. As my friends and family will tell you, I'm normally a very calm guy who's content to let life flow by him undisturbed. But every now and then, something gets my goat, and that's when I go off.

I remember one occasion as if it were yesterday. I had set up an appointment with a client—someone with whom I'd not had a lot of contact—and we'd agreed on a Tuesday afternoon meeting. He was someone I'd sized up as a bit of a challenge, even before our first real conversation. First, his company had experienced rapid growth and had risen to be the leader of its particular niche. So there was a measure of arrogance involved.

Second, he was short. Now, because I'm short, I know that there's a tendency for short people to compensate for their lack of inches by being extra-aggressive. And that was the case with this guy. He was a bit more than five foot four inches tall, but his tendency was to act as if he were seven feet six and played forward for the Los Angeles Lakers. From the minute we spoke on the phone to set up the appointment, I had a feeling I was going to be put through the wringer with this guy.

This was combined with the fact that the appointment came at a time of something of a crossroads for me. I was considering, for the first time in a long while, selling the company that I'd created and built from scratch. It felt as if I were putting a child up for adoption. I knew it was the right decision, but that didn't make it any easier. The day before meeting with this client, I'd had the first of what would prove to be many meetings with the representatives of the company that—full disclosure here—finally bought the company.

So, to say I was feeling emotionally torn the day of my meeting with the client is putting it mildly. I'd felt too upset to eat breakfast, and I was buzzing on four cups of coffee, two of them hyped-up extra strong with shots of espresso. I swept into his office as if I owned the place and plopped down in a chair with all the authority of Louis XVI pulling up a seat at Versailles on a morning when his ministers had been particularly annoying.

The client, perhaps in response to my mood, was in the spirit of Napoleon. He was ready to re-fight Austerlitz. Hell, he was ready to re-invade Russia!

My memory of the occasion is a bit muddled, but I know how it ended: with the two of us yelling at one another, our faces red, and our voices hoarse. I stamped out of the meeting, slamming the door, prepared to swear that never, in a thousand years, would I talk to this guy again.

NEVER'S A LONG TIME

And the upshot? Well, you guessed it. A year or so later, the client and I were having dinner in a nice restaurant. The wine was good, the steak with bearnaise sauce was excellent, and I felt compelled to ask him: Why didn't you just go somewhere else? What would make you interested in ever doing business with me again?

He took a sip of Pinot Noir and thought about it. Then he leaned forward.

"I'll tell you what, Steve," he said. "I thought about it. I really did. But there was one thing that kept me focused on finishing the deal."

"What was that?"

"I needed what you were selling."

That's really the big lesson of this chapter. You may get angry, and your client may get angry, but if at the end of the day your client needs what you're selling, you can still close the deal. What you need is a positive attitude and an understanding of the dynamics of the situation.

You may think it's odd that I've chosen to start this chapter about how to sell to an angry client with an account of how I was angry and almost blew a sale. But please understand: The difference between you having a temper fit and your client getting ticked off isn't that great. The art of selling to an angry client is this: *You must be able to see things from his side.*

In my experience, clients express anger for one of four reasons:

1. **You'd done/said something stupid.** Much as I'd like to reassure you that in the course of your career you're never going to tick off a client, I'm afraid that's impossible. There are almost an infinite number of things you can say or do to make a client mad at you, and at some point in your career I'm afraid you'd going to experience all of them. It's not that this is deliberate on your part. But when you see your client's lips compress to a line that you could mark with a ruler and her fingers start to clench as if they're strangling baby rabbits, you need to quickly review what you've just said and figure out why it's ringing her bells.

2. **Sometimes no means no.** I believe, and I've expressed this belief in an earlier chapter, that an objection is an

opportunity. But sometimes, when the client says no, he really means no. You need to recognize that and be able to convert it into a forward-pointing closure. Something along the lines of, "Well, I can understand why you don't want to do business with us right now, but I think it's essential that we keep in touch. Here's my phone number and e-mail. Can we set up another time to talk next Tuesday at 2 PM?"

3. **The client is probably mad at someone other than you.** Here's a piece of amateur psychology, derived from nearly fifty years of observing the human species: If someone gets irrationally angry at you, it's probably because the person is angry about something else in her or his life. In my years in sales, I've found this a remarkably useful piece of information. When I'm sitting down with a client and she suddenly explodes all over me like a Fourth of July rocket, chances are that she's mad about something else and is taking it out on me. As long as I can keep that in mind, it's possible to salvage something from the sales call.

4. **What do you really have to be angry about?** I mean, really? What you're doing isn't brain surgery. If you screw up, no one dies. So just take a chill pill (this, I'm informed, is the correct jargon in these situations). Relax. It's not the end of the world if you don't make the sale.

The curious thing is that the more you relax and don't take a "My way or the highway" attitude, the more likely you are to actually complete the sale. At a minimum, you'll find that the client will continue to talk to you, which is more than half the battle.

With all this in mind, let's go back to the situation we encountered at the start of this chapter. How could I have handled the client's anger differently?

IT'S NOT ABOUT YOU

To begin with, I could have recognized that his anger was not really directed at me. In fact, I could have started from the standpoint that any good salesperson should begin from: The sales call is about the client. No one else counts.

This isn't just a moral call. It's a practical recognition that as a salesperson you are nothing without the client. Your first and most important job is to engage him in discussion. Until you've done that, the sale hasn't even begun.

"But after all," I can hear you say, "isn't the problem that he wants to dominate the sale? Doesn't he want to dictate the terms on which you'll conclude the deal?"

Probably. But the point is that once we get a discussion going, it's possible for me to engage him in a negotiation. Until that happens, nothing's going on. Once we start talking, we can figure out what works best for both of us. And then, his anger will dissolve.

SCENARIO

Let's see how this works in practice.

> *Client*: I don't see what we even have to talk about. I don't have time for this.

> *Salesperson*: I can certainly understand why you're upset about the state of industry right now. It would probably help me if you were to explain two or three of the major challenges you see at the moment that your company has to overcome.

> *Client*: Well, all right, if you really want to hear.

Salesperson: I think it would be a great benefit in understanding why you're at this crossroads and how my company can help you.

Note that in this conversation the salesperson does not challenge the client's assumptions; there's no point in that. The client believes what she believes. It's much more important for you, the salesperson, to establish a rapport with her and understand her point of view. Her anger is really a function at this point of the anger she feels about the situation she's been put in: Her industry is under attack, and she's got to defend it.

The salesperson doesn't try to set himself up in opposition to her viewpoint. Instead, he sympathizes with her and suggests that if she'll explain the problem in more detail, he may be able to help. This is the key to getting a sale out of this situation: The salesperson must present himself as someone who's able to help solve the problem the client is facing.

THE OUT-OF-CONTROL CLIENT

Every now and then, a client gets completely beyond your capacity to help. It's not that she's angry with someone else; she's gotten to the point where she can't recognize the sources of her anger, and all she can do is vent.

Here, the important thing is to understand the limits of your capacity. You're not a psychologist, and you shouldn't try to be one. If the client has gotten to a state in which she is not able to accept your help, move on and recommend that she receive professional assistance.

I've had, over the years, several clients whom I finally had to recommend for clinical help. None of them recognized that they needed it, and with two exceptions none of them sought it. But I don't stay up nights worrying about it. I truly believe that at the end of the day, you do what you want to do. If you want to recover from a problem, you'll find a way to do it.

Clients who get angry with you and refuse to listen to a reasoned argument aren't likely to change even if you find more facts and figures with which to challenge their assumptions. At a certain point you've got to stop trying and move on with your life. My recommendation is that you develop a good sense of when a client is being angry and when she is going out on a limb she'll not crawl back from. The success in recognizing the difference will help you make the difference in your professional life between success and failure.

THE PASSIVE-AGGRESSIVE CLIENT

24

I swear the following scenario is true:

Salesperson: Let's discuss delivery times. Our warehouse ships on the second Tuesday of every month. How does that work for you?

Client: The second Tuesday is pretty bad.

Salesperson: Okay. We can probably work around that. What's a good time for you?

Client: Oh, the second Tuesday can work.

Salesperson: But you just said it was really bad.

Client: No, no. We can make it work.

Salesperson: Okay. So the second Tuesday of every month then?

Client: Yeah, yeah. But that's not really very good for us.

Salesperson: What's a good time for you?

Client: Oh, whatever you like.

If you're like me, this scenario will send you into the outer reaches of damnation. It's not just that the client is being problematic about nailing down a date; after all, who hasn't dealt with indecision before? It's that every time you think you've come to an agreement it slips away from you.

The sure sign of a passive-aggressive client.

AGGRESSIVE BEHAVIOR AS A TACTIC

Over the years I've encountered my fair share (I might say, *more* than my fair share, but who's counting?) of these kinds of clients. They're among my least favorite people to deal with because there never seems to be anything to fight. As you may have guessed from some of the anecdotes in these pages, I can be a pretty aggressive sort of guy, ready to fight to back up my opinions.

But what do you do when the opinion you're fighting against has no more substantiality than a will o' the wisp? What do you do when you step down decisively on the stair and it isn't there?

The first thing to do is to recognize that what you're facing is a negotiation and sales tactic. Passive-aggressive people don't always behave that way on purpose. But for you, it's best to assume that they know what they're doing and what effect they're trying to achieve. Passive-aggressive behavior is always calculated to get you to make the first move.

This is understandable. It's much easier in any situation to be reactive rather than proactive. You can make your opposite number come to you if you constantly fight from a defensive rather than an offensive position (more on this point later on). The essence of passive aggressiveness is to wrong-foot you by forcing you to always be the one proposing things.

SCENARIO

Again, consider the following situation:

Salesperson: Now let's move on to price.

Client: Price isn't really as important as quality, is it?

Salesperson: Do you think quality is the most important thing we should talk about? We can offer some guarantees that will make this attractive.

Client: Oh, I'm not saying that quality is the *most* important thing. But I don't think you should ignore it.

Salesperson: I'm not ignoring it, I'm—

Client: I just don't understand why it's not important to you. I would think that this would be something you'd emphasize.

Salesperson: No, it's completely important. And we're willing to make a guarantee that—

Client: That's going to come with a price, though, isn't it? And price is pretty important to us.

Salesperson: Well . . .

Sadly, in the next moment the salesperson's head explodes.

Not really, but you get the idea. Notice the degree to which the client in this scenario has controlled the conversation. Every turn has been because of something she has proposed. The salesperson, unfortunately, has allowed the discussion to get completely out of his hands.

As I've said earlier in this and in my other books, it's essential in sales to follow the 80/20 rule in selling: The client should do 80 percent of the talking, and the salesperson should do 20 percent. From this you may have gotten the idea that in some way the client should determine the direction of the discussion. But this isn't the case at all. In fact, it's you who should control the conversation. You just have to do it without talking.

What's that? It probably sounds like nonsense. Who can control a conversation by talking *less?*

Well, you can. Because a sales discussion isn't about the amount you talk. It's about what you say. And by recognizing the features of passive aggression early on, you can see how to move the discussion past them.

THE FEATURES OF PASSIVE-AGGRESSIVE BEHAVIOR

The essential point here is to understand what you're dealing with. People who are passive aggressive are not seeking to find a solution to their problem. Instead, they're trying to establish power over your dialogue so they can make you do what they want. The quicker you understand this, the faster you'll be able to counter their tactics.

What should you look for to define a passive-aggressive personality?

1. Passive-aggressive types apparently look to you to make decisions. If you're in a conversation in which you feel as if you're always being pushed to take the initiative by the other party, step back a few paces and ask, Is this a passive-aggressive personality? Always remember that the key word is "apparently." In reality, passive-aggressive people want to force a decision on you.

2. Passive aggressives hate decisions. The more you try to push them to make a firm commitment to buy, the more

they'll back off. If you're trying to get a buy decision out of a client and she just keeps scuttling backward, it's possible you've got a passive aggressive on your hands.

3. Passive aggressives constantly shift the topic. One of the key features of any sales discussion is that it should stay on topic. Oh, you can veer from side to side now and then, but in general you want the client to stay focused on a limited range of things, chiefly: How can you help him solve his problem? If he keeps trying to change the subject of the discussion, it's possible that he's passive aggressive.

Passive aggressiveness isn't always a conscious tactic; it can also be a way of life for some people. Several years ago I knew a guy who in every situation instinctively reverted to this kind of behavior. I was in a restaurant one time with him when he managed to drag out negotiations with the waiter over a drinks bill for forty-five minutes (interestingly enough, he left without paying his bar bill—he'd convinced the waiter it just wasn't worth it to argue with him). He was absolutely convinced he was demanding no more than what was coming to him and that he would never dream of cheating anyone out of something that wasn't rightfully his.

From maintaining a friendship with this guy—and believe me, there were times when it wasn't easy—over twenty or more years, I learned some valuable lessons about dealing with passive-aggressive personalities. They've served me well over the years in sales.

First, the thing passive-aggressive people *don't* want to do is make a decision. They want you to do it, and they want it to be the wrong one, so they can reject it. The answer is to be decisive and forceful in choosing an alternative. Dithering gets you nowhere—it's simply playing their game. You need to pick a road and go down it with a brisk step. Sure, it may be wrong, but at least it looks as if you intend to do what you're doing. As my old music teacher used to say, "If you're going to make a mistake, make it loudly!"

Second, take control of the discussion. This means demanding the floor and holding it against all other attempts to regain it. There's no need for rudeness. Instead, you can hold the lead in a conversation by doing what I've advocated in this and all my other books: asking questions. Think about the following exchange:

Client: I'm not really sure about this issue of functionality.

Salesperson: I'm sorry to hear that. What's bothering you about it?

Client: Nothing, really. But I just don't know.

Salesperson: Well, if something's bothering you, we should talk about it now. After all, it's much better to have this discussion now than six months from now when your warehouse is filled with these products. So, what's bothering you about the functionality?

Client: Nothing. Forget I mentioned it.

Salesperson: I wish I could do that. But I think this is something important that we should resolve before we go any further. Can you tell me something the product doesn't do that you need it to do?

Client: No, I guess not. Don't worry about it.

Salesperson: Well, if you're not worried about it, I certainly won't. But just to make sure, how about if we institute some specific quality control tests six months from now to make sure all your concerns have been met?

Here the client has tried to imply, without quite saying it, that there's something wrong with the product's quality. The salesperson simply won't let the issue go. He proposes a specific series of tests of the product's quality. This puts the burden of the matter back on the client, who must now demonstrate a specific area in which the product or service falls short.

GET A DECISION

The biggest challenge that the passive-aggressive client may pose to you is your inability to get him to make a freaking decision. This is where your patience tests its outer limits. I mean, how hard is it to decide on a course of action that will, in the long run, benefit you and your organization? Just sign on the dotted line, for Chrissakes, and let's get this over with!

It might seem like that—particularly when the client isn't inclined to sign in the first place. But keep your hat on. You'll need to ease the client toward a signature. Shouting and pointing fingers isn't going to help things at present.

There are a couple of things you can do to push the client toward a decision:

1. **Position yourself as being on the client's side against the unnamed Powers That Be.** You can say something along the lines of, "I understand completely that you don't want to make a commitment right now, but unfortunately, my boss insists that he has to have all sales orders in by this Friday so he can pull together the numbers for the quarter. I know how inconvenient that is for you, and I apologize."

2. **Don't say anything.** As I've mentioned elsewhere in this book (and in other books), silence is a very powerful weapon. When you don't talk, the other party has a tendency to talk in order to fill the void. And for a passive-aggressive personality, talking can lead to a resolution.

One final point: The more you study passive-aggressive people and try to get inside their heads, the more successful you're likely to be in coming up with tactics to counter them. With experience, you'll be able to face even the most annoying client with confidence and a positive attitude.

THE INDECISIVE
CLIENT

25

M y friend Bob told me this story. It happened to him quite a long time ago—about thirty years or so, when he was starting out in the sales business. He was young, eager, and enthusiastic, full of the power of positive selling. It so happened that one of his accounts was with a large company that had recently undergone a shake-up in management. The result was that the buyer was someone nobody in Bob's firm had heard of before, let alone dealt with.

Bob made an appointment with the buyer and pulled together research on the company. He compiled a stack of photocopies of the firm's annual reports, sales figures gleaned from various sources, and background information on the company based on scanning newspaper and magazine articles. He wrote up the material, studied it, and thought out his approach to the sales call. He knew that the account was an important one, so he didn't want to leave anything to chance.

The day of the call, he was up bright and early, ate a good, balanced breakfast to keep his energy at peak, and set out on his drive to the meeting. The sun was shining, there wasn't a cloud to be seen, and the sky was that kind of deep blue that looks like it goes on forever. Bob whistled as he drove. He tells me that in his recollection of the morning, even the other drivers on the road were smiling as they passed him.

Everything, in short, was set to go his way.

He got to the company's headquarters and was greeted by a charming administrative assistant. She fetched him a cup of delicious steaming coffee, and he sat sipping it, waiting for the executive to show up. Five minutes passed. Then ten minutes. Bob checked his watch and stuck his head out the door.

"Anything delaying Mr. Smith?" he asked the admin.

"I'm sorry he's not here yet," she replied. "He'll be along in a minute. He's sometimes a bit late to meetings."

Another five minutes passed. Bob checked and rechecked the materials he'd laid out on the table. He strolled to the window and stared down at the cars lining the parking lot. Then he paced back and forth across the room several times. Finally, he put his head out of the door and smiled at the admin, who smiled back.

"I'm sure he'll be here *any* minute," she said.

Just then the elevator doors rolled back and the executive in question hurried in. His hair was slightly ruffled, and he gave off the air of someone who's passed through a high wind. He nodded distractedly to Bob, asked the admin for messages, and was about to disappear into his office when the admin motioned with her head in the direction of Bob, standing patiently in the doorway of the conference room.

"Oh. Right. Sure. Just a minute."

Mr. Smith moved in the direction of his office and then hesitated and turned. "No. Let's talk now." He bustled into the conference room and sat down at the long table. "Okay. Let's get . . ." He stopped, looked at his watch, then jumped to his feet. "No, let me just . . ." He started toward the door, stopped, and returned to his seat. "Just give me the short version, please," he said.

Now Bob was feeling anxious, as if some of Mr. Smith's nervousness had somehow slipped beneath his collar. He shuffled through his notes, feeling disorganized and confused. Finally he found an appropriate starting place and began his pitch. As with all good pitches, it was full of questions, starting with:

"Mr. Smith, what would you say are the main challenges your industry faces right now?"

Mr. Smith looked as if someone had asked him to explain quantum mechanics in three sentences. Bob, who's from New York, hadn't had a lot of experience with wildlife, but he told me afterward that he understood at that moment what the expression "Deer in the headlights" meant. Mr. Smith stumbled over a few sentences, contradicted himself, went back and explained the contradiction, and then managed to choke out, "What do you think?"

I won't go into detail about the rest of the call. Suffice it to say that at the end, when Bob—who by this time was feeling as if he'd rather have been anywhere else than that conference room—asked Mr. Smith to confirm the deal, Mr. Smith, after some hemming and hawing, shook his head.

"I just don't think I'm ready to make a decision about this today," he said. "Could we take this up some other time?"

Bob gathered up the threads of his rapidly fraying temper. "Sure," he agreed. "How about next Tuesday at 10?"

"No, Tuesday's no good."

"Wednesday?"

"No, I don't think so. I'll have to get back to you and work something out."

And that's where Bob left things.

A PATTERN OF INDECISION

Driving back through a sudden squall of driving rain, facing drivers who, he told me, were all scowling and doing their best to push him to the side of the road, Bob reviewed what had gone wrong. Clearly, he thought, he was looking at a pattern—from Mr. Smith's tardiness in arriving at the meeting to his obvious lack of organization. The heart of the matter, though, was that Mr. Smith was afraid, terrified, really, to make a decision.

It was a curious situation because you'd think that among the qualities a company looks for among in its executives, decision-making would be one of the first. After all, executives are called that because of what they do: They *execute*. They take the decisions reached by the various higher bodies of the corporation, and they make them a reality. In order to do that, they have to make hundreds, if not thousands of decisions every day, ranging from the great to the small.

So an indecisive executive is actually a pretty rare breed in corporate America. Nonetheless, they do occur. When you have the misfortune to run up against a master of indecision, as Bob had, the consequences to your sales call may be disastrous.

It's important to stress what Bob did right in this situation:

When Mr. Smith was late, Bob didn't simply storm out of the office in exasperation. Nor, when Mr. Smith finally showed up, did Bob berate him for his lateness. That kind of thing won't get a sales call off on the right foot. Instead, Bob strove to stress a positive attitude: He was there to help.

When Mr. Smith asked Bob to cut his presentation short, the salesperson didn't do either of the things that were tempting: tell Mr. Smith to go to hell or simply ignore him and start at the beginning of his set presentation. Instead, he tried to go for a shorter version of the pitch.

When Mr. Smith couldn't make a decision about the deal and asked for more time to think about it, Bob proposed a specific day and time for a follow up meeting.

What else could Bob have done to turn things around?

I stress here that one aspect of positive selling is the ability to think on your feet. In any given situation in the field, you can expect things to change quickly. It helps, when sitting in the office before a sales call, to envision some of the major things that could go wrong. Still, you can only imagine a limited number of scenarios. So you've got to fall back on the basic principles of positive selling.

1. **You're there to help the client.** In this case, the client, Mr. Smith, has trouble making a decision. You can't make the decision for him, but you need to find out what information he needs to come to a conclusion. So one thing Bob could have asked is if there was any further information Mr. Smith needed him to compile and send.

2. **It's essential to keep the discussion moving forward.** The problem with indecisive people is that they tend to let conversations stall. The solution, from the salesperson's point of view, is to find something about which the executive feels comfortable making a decision. Usually, this is something small, but it sets a pattern. If you can get the executive to agree, for instance, on the date of a follow up meeting, it'll be easier to get him to agree to an aspect of the deal you're trying to make. So Bob could have pushed for a follow up time and date earlier in the meeting.

3. **A sales call that starts down a bad track will, all things being equal, continue on that track until it crashes.** You can call this the Schiffman Law of Bad Sales. Once your train has gone off the tracks, it's very unlikely that it'll get back on if you just keep going. The solution is to find another tactic, one that will alter the character and/or momentum of the conversation. In this case, Bob could have tried to slow down the discussion, possibly by diverting it temporarily onto another topic. Once you've changed the subject or the pace, everyone has a chance to think a bit more calmly and reflectively, and things can get back to where they should be.

I didn't mention any of this to Bob when he told me the story—it would have felt too much like twisting the dagger in the wound. In fact, I didn't even think of some of this until after listening to a number of similar experiences over the years. But it's convinced me of something important: *An indecisive client is essentially someone who wants to make a decision but wants help in making it.*

Again, you can't make the decision for the client. The client doesn't want you to do it, and in any case, it may very well be counteracted at higher levels of the company. But you can, nonetheless, help. Take these steps:

1. Slow down. Take a break or change the subject for a minute.

2. Break the deal proposition down into small parts and review them.

3. Get the client to make a small decision about one of the parts.

4. Stress the value of that small decision.

5. Get as many decisions as you can concerning the parts of the deal.

6. Agree to temporarily shelve the other parts.

7. Ask what help you can give, information you can provide, or anything else the client wants.

8. Set a time and place for your next meeting.

Above all, there's no reason for impatience. Too many salespeople seem to think that if you can't close the deal in the first meeting, you've failed. That's nonsense. Some deals take weeks or months of patient negotiation, and they can't be rushed. Often what's at the heart of such deals is a lot of complexity, but sometimes it's the reluctance of the people involved to commit themselves to a firm decision. If that's the case, take your time and give them what they need. Do that and you'll find that the birds will still be singing when you come out of the meeting, and the sky will still be blue and cloudless.

THE NEEDY CLIENT

26

I've always been a dog person. From a very early point in my life, I've been surrounded by dogs, and over the course of many years I've had a variety of canine friends. I don't say this to insult cat owners in any way—I'm well aware of the passion that dogs and cats inspire in people, and I remain largely agnostic on the issue of whether dogs or cats are man's best friend. In the interests of full disclosure, though, I should state that I'm allergic to cats and can't get anywhere near them without sneezing my head off. Thus on the whole, I have to say I prefer the company of dogs.

At present, I have two. One, a ten-year-old black terrier, is compact and self-reliant. He knows what he wants and doesn't demand anything from me, except on the rare occasions when something irritates him (like thunder), in which case he wants to make sure I know he's not happy.

The other is five years old. A golden retriever, she's a delicate princess of an animal. When she enters a room, she pushes her nose into it, sniffs the air, and flicks her paw into the air, as if to say, "Not quite up to my standards, but it will have to do for now."

You'd think, with all that, she'd be the more independent of the two. But in fact, she's the epitome of neediness. At night, she flops down at the foot of the bed. (My wife draws the line at the idea of her sleeping on the bed. Very sensibly, since otherwise she—the dog, that is—takes over all the available space and spreads out like a blanket.) Every morning, at the crack of dawn, she's at her food dish, howling in a voice that could shatter glass at twenty paces. Once breakfast has been served to her majesty, she's pawing at the front door, demanding that I get on with it and take her for her morning walk. She nods politely to the doorman on the way out the front door and tugs eagerly at the leash, wanting to explore the world at large.

After about five minutes of this, I'm pretty well done, but she's just getting started. She wants to run around the block, trying for a new Olympic record. I draw the line at this, and we finish in a close race at the front door. By that time, I'm ready to go back to bed. She shrugs and curls up, softly muttering to herself.

WHEN THE CLIENT DEMANDS ATTENTION

I mention all of this because it seems to me that neediness, whether in a dog or in a human, operates on pretty much the same set of principles. (I'm sure all of you who are cat lovers have similar stories to tell about the felines in your life.) The focus has to be on them, and it doesn't matter how many other things you've got going on, they're the center of the universe and your big accomplishment in life.

Not that long ago I had a client who, in a previous life, probably *was* a cat, if such things are measured by neediness. It started at our first conversation.

"Steve," he said to me, "I want you to know that I've got some concerns about the training program we've signed you on for."

"Okay," I replied. "Why don't you tell me what they are?"

He launched into a ten-minute exposition of what sounded like a blow-by-blow description of the crash of the *Hindenberg*. By the time he was done, I was left to wonder why on earth he'd inked the deal, since it was clear he was terrified of the awful consequences it might have for his business. I spent forty minutes soothing him and assuring him that he'd see practical, measurable results within six months of my training his sales force. I left with a feeling of a job accomplished, albeit at the cost of my nervous system.

The next day he called me. "I've been thinking about what you said," he opened, "and I've still got some concerns." We spent another thirty minutes on the phone. From then on it was a pattern. Every couple of days he'd call with a new issue or problem. I'd utter soothing phrases, he'd slowly climb back off the window ledge, and eventually I'd hang up the phone with an increasing conviction that it was just going to be a matter of forty-eight hours before I was right back where I started.

Gradually I came to realize a fundamental truth about dealing with this client, one that can be extended to most clients in this category: When you talk to people like this, you're not dealing with problems that can be resolved on a rational basis. Instead, you're trying to answer a very deep, complicated psychological need, and the response that the client is demanding is emotional, not rational.

In considering the philosophy of positive selling, I've spent a lot of time thinking about this particular problem, because it doesn't seem to fit some of the other things I've told you over the years about selling. Selling, to me, is about finding out the client's problems and figuring out what you can do to find a solution. Then it's about presenting that solution in a compelling way to the client, answering his objections, and explaining the specific benefits that my product or service will provide. All in all, a rational process.

But a needy client is concerned, above all, with emotion. He wants you to respond on an emotional level. As a positive salesperson, you've got to be prepared to do that. But—and this is a very big point—you don't have to respond on the level the needy client is demanding. In fact, you shouldn't.

Someone who demands constant attention from you does so because he has a significant need that's not being fulfilled. And he believes from past experience that a strategy of neediness will work. Harking back for a moment to my dog, she wants my attention in the morning because she knows that if she complains long enough, I'll give in and take her for a walk. (My wife, I should say, is not a partner to my indulgence and thinks that if we ignore the damn dog, she'll shut up. I pay attention to the dog rather than to my wife, because the dog is louder.) So the first step in solving the problem of a needy client is to not do what he wants you to do: Pay attention.

When my needy client called, wanting to talk to me for the upteenth time about the concerns he had that his sales force's delicate balance might be upset by the training I'd scheduled, at a certain point I stopped returning his phone calls. I let him stew for about five days before calling him back. In other words, I disrupted his pattern of behavior.

When I spoke to him, he was bubbling over with anger and resentment. But at that point, he'd fallen out of the normal pattern of wanting attention. Now he wanted something else: a solution and an apology.

I was unprepared to give him the second. But I told him flat out, "Look, based on past experience, the training I'm going to give your salespeople will include the following effects:

1.   It will improve their cold call ratio by X percent.

2.   It will increase the number of cold calls they make in a given week by Y percent.

3.   It will increase the number of closes they make by Z percent.

I made those three promises to him and then I said, "If you don't see these results within a six-month period, measured by statistical analysis, I'll drop the rest of the training program and I won't charge you for what I've done already."

I didn't believe it was much of a risk on my part, because after a lot of years in the field I know down pat what results I can expect from my training. But what it did was give him something very specific to react to. I took the discussion from the level of general, "I'm concerned about this" to "I'll promise this, and if I don't deliver, you can fire me."

The results were what I expected. He hemmed and hawed a bit and then agreed to what I was proposing. From an emotional point of view, he was encountering a strong counterpoint, and he gave way in front of it.

That's not to say that he gave up entirely the pattern of needy behavior. It was too strongly ingrained in his personality, and I still got more phone calls from him than from most of my other clients put together. But now we'd broken the general pattern of the calls. Rather than constantly find this, that, or the other point to complain about or ask about, he had specific, promised statistics to check against. And, as one after the other, these goals were met by my program, his concerns became less and less.

THE ANSWER TO THE NEEDY CLIENT

All of this is to say that the best answer to neediness is specifics. Make promises, but make them quantifiable. And be sure they're promises you can fulfill. Remember one of the commandments of Positive Selling: *It's better to under-promise and over-deliver.* Scale back your promises and work like mad to deliver more than the client is expecting. Any client who is needy will be impressed by such actions.

Needy clients are often that way precisely because they expect you to deliver less than you promise. They're convinced that the only way they can get you to respond is by constant nagging. My dog works on very much that principle, assuming that just because she's been fed every morning for five years, today could well be the day that she's not fed and starves.

At the same time, I want to stress that it's easier and better to have needy clients than indifferent ones. I've on occasion encountered clients who just couldn't be bothered to find out what I could do for them. They were convinced that their business— and mine—was going to hell in a handbasket and nothing could be done about it. Such clients are also focused on an emotional, rather than a rational, response, but the range of what you can do is much less. No matter how many problems you solve for them, it's never good enough. As far as they're concerned, the industry—indeed, the whole economy—is always collapsing and they're just trying to get out of the way. In most cases, I believe this pathology is terminal. If people don't want to be helped, you can't help them.

This leads me to a final point. I believe strongly in what I might call one of the fundamental principles of Schiffman's Philosophy of Selling: People do what they want to do.

That is to say, as a salesperson, all you're doing is urging people in the direction they have a natural tendency to take. Someone who wants to make his business a success will do whatever it takes for that to happen. A client who wants to conquer an industry through brilliant innovative moves will acquire the skills and the drive to do that. So with needy clients, one of the first fundamental questions you need to ask yourself is: Does this person really want to be helped? If he does, your way is clear.

COMING TO
A CLOSE

27

Closing a sale has its own peculiar set of challenges. (I should know. I've written a bestselling book, *Closing Techniques* [*That Really Work!*]) Nothing illustrates this better than a story a friend of mine told me.

My friend—I'll call him John—and his wife, Mary, were buying a house. This was back when house-buying was a lot less complicated and stressful than it is today in the wake of the 2008 recession, and John and Mary had found a place they really liked. They talked to their realtor and put in an offer.

The owners counter-offered, and my friends countered the counter. All perfectly normal and part of the give and take that goes into house buying. John and Mary, meanwhile, assuming that matters would be swiftly concluded, gave their landlord notice and began piling their belongings in boxes. They asked their realtor to let them know the minute he heard from the selling party so they could set up a convenient closing date.

A week slipped by, then ten days, and a small, persistent alarm bell started to ring in the back of John's mind. He contacted the realtor. No, the other party hadn't been in touch. Moreover, their realtor had not been returning calls. John's realtor was getting very concerned.

John and Mary returned to their packing, though with notably less enthusiasm. Another four days went by, and then the phone rang. It was their realtor, with good and bad news. The good news was that the sellers' representative had finally called him back. The bad news was that the sellers had imposed a raft of new conditions on the sale, including bumping up the price by $5,000.

At this point, John and Mary were in a tough position. They'd given notice to quit their apartment, and finding another on short notice wouldn't be easy. Emotionally, they'd committed to their new house, making detailed plans about where to put their furniture, how to fix up the yard, and a thousand other things. With great reluctance and after some significant soul-searching, they told their realtor they'd accept the new terms.

The day was set for the closing, and all the parties gathered in a lawyer's offices to sign the papers. Sitting across from the sellers—who, John told me later, were looking intolerably smug and self-satisfied—John felt his temper slipping away from him. As he reached out for the final papers in the deal, he snapped out a comment. The seller replied with another. John hit back.

A few minutes later, unsigned papers were shoved to the middle of the table, John was out of the room by one door while the seller was slamming the other. Both realtors were sitting at the table with their heads in their hands.

Surprisingly, this sort of thing isn't as uncommon in the real estate business as you might think. I spoke to another friend of mine about it, one who's a realtor, and he said that although it's unusual, virtually anyone who's been in the business more than a decade or so has seen at least one sale blow up at closing.

THE POWER OF UNRESOLVED ISSUES

I asked about this topic a bit more, and he made a comment that stayed with me as good advice to salespeople looking to close deals. "Closing," he said, "is a time when unresolved issues are all pushed to the surface."

I thought about that and concluded that it's true. There's a tendency sometimes when we're in the middle of a complex sale to put off or bury questions and concerns in order to focus on the main points of agreement. I think, on the whole, this is a good strategy. One of the aspects of positive selling is to focus on what you agree on, rather than get bogged down in disagreements about smaller issues. That said, though, before you close the deal, you're going to have to resolve pretty much all the issues that have come up in the course of the sale. Because if you don't, there are two places they're going to reappear: the closing and during contract-signing.

Here's the odd thing. If they come up at either of these two points, it's quite possible that they'll assume an importance quite out of proportion to their real significance. It's possible that they can sink the sale altogether, even if you and the client are in basic agreement on the big questions.

How should you approach these issues, then?

1. Follow my advice from earlier in this book, and don't get hung up on small questions. Get alignment first on the big issues. Sometimes the smaller questions will simply go away when you do this.

2. After each meeting with the client, send a follow up e-mail summarizing what you discussed, what you agreed on, what were points of disagreement, and what issues were left unresolved or un-discussed. This will do away with the problem of smaller questions getting forgotten until the closing.

3. In between sales calls, review the unresolved questions and come up with solutions.

THE COURAGE TO CLOSE

A second, related problem that interferes with closing results from what I might call a lack of courage (or, at least, initiative) on the part of salespeople: They're scared to close. This is precisely because they know that the closing is where they're going to have to deal with these unresolved problems. This is where the rubber hits the road and both parties have to make a specific, written commitment to a set of actions.

As a result, I've seen some salespeople go round and round, churning up the same sections of ground, never asking the client to sign on the line. Their subconscious reasoning is that as long as they don't close, they don't have to have a potentially unpleasant confrontation with the client.

To those people, let me say: There's no way to put this off. The longer you postpone it, the worse it will be. The trick is to learn to read the signs about when it's best to close and when the sale still has a way to run.

Harking back to my friends John and Mary, there were obvious signs that the sale was in trouble. The fact that the other party went silent for a period of time and the outrageous set of conditions that were part of the counteroffer—both these developments should have told them that they needed to start considering alternatives. In sales parlance, this is called the Best Alternative to a Negotiated Agreement, or BATNA. I prefer just to think of it as finding a reasonable alternative. Among the questions John and Mary should have asked themselves were:

1. If we don't buy the house, where can we live for a reasonable amount of money until such time as we can find another house we want to buy?

2. What middle ground can we find between what we want to pay and what the seller is demanding?

3. What is the seller hoping to gain by these demands?

In the same way, during the course of a sale—which may take several weeks or several months, depending on its size and complexity—you should be alert for signs that the deal is going off the rails. When those signs appear, start asking questions about your alternatives. Don't wait for the closing to do so—if you do, you'll be in a weaker position, because the client will know that you've committed to the sale and need it to come through. Remember this: The person at the closing who holds the stronger hand will find that fact increase because it's the closing. In other words, an advantage in a sale is stronger when it appears at the closing.

Precisely for this reason, you should carefully review the best time to close and calculate that timing so that you close when you hold the strongest cards in your hand. There's nothing dishonest or underhanded about this. It's simply a matter of making sure that the deal closes in the best possible way for you and your company.

ELEMENTS OF A GOOD CLOSE

A bad close is easy enough to identify: It's when both you and client walk away from the meeting hoping that you never have to talk to one another again. I've made plenty of bad closes in my time, and believe me, most of the time your gut will give you ample warning when you've made a bad deal.

What are the main parts of a good close?

1. **Both you and the client feel good about the deal.** You can both clearly see the upside of it, and you understand and are excited by the opportunities it offers.

2. **There are no significant unresolved issues.**

3. **Both of you clearly understand the terms of the deal.** This is going to come up again at the contract stage, when you and your legal team will carefully review the terms of the sale, so it's essential that you and the client not have any

surprises. If there's any ambiguity in your mind, it's good to resolve it before completing the close.

4. **The deal has set up a future, ongoing relationship.**
   I believe firmly that each individual sale is a brick in the larger edifice of a strong relationship with your client. A one-time sale is just that: good for one time only, and of limited benefit. A successful close should set the stage for a long, productive relationship between you and the client.

Particularly in light of this last point, it's important that when you close a deal, you set up a time for a follow up meeting. After all, you want to make sure that everything about the deal is going well and that there are no significant problems.

John told me that six months after the purchase of the house blew up in everyone's face, he and Mary bought another house. The sale went like a dream; their counteroffer was accepted, there were no surprise issues that came up at the closing, and he and Mary loved the new house at least as much as, if not more than, the one they'd lost to the sellers' obstinacy.

What also impressed him was that both his realtor and the realtor representing the sellers called him a month after the sale to make sure he and Mary were happy in their new home. He told me that this sort of thing was what convinced him that should they ever move again, they'll use the same realtor. In other words, the realtor, by a simple phone call, set up a long-term relationship that could, in the future, lead to another significant commission. It's that easy.

WHEN TO
WALK AWAY

28

My exposure to poker has been extremely limited, both by inexperience and by my own innate caution. I completely understand the attraction of playing for high stakes in Las Vegas, Reno, or similar places. It's just that when I think about waging anything more than two or three dollars on a hand, my palms start to sweat.

A few years ago, I visited Atlantic City and watched people playing poker. The stakes even then weren't especially high—the kitty never, as far as I could tell, got much above $50—but I found that after five minutes I had to turn away. I just couldn't deal with it.

At such times, I remember the advice from professional gamblers (the sort who show up on television playing in the World Series of Poker). In a lifetime of studying the habits of their opponents, their approach is actually pretty simple. They say that the most important part of a winning poker strategy is knowing when to keep what you've got and when to fold. In addition, there are times when a successful gambler has to know when to walk away from the table. And that, I suspect, is one reason poker makes me nervous: I'm not convinced I've got the willpower to walk away from the table at the right time.

GET YOUR TIMING RIGHT

In sales, timing is everything. A professional gambler would say, "You've got to know when to keep your hand." That is to say, you've got to know when you're in a strong position in a sale and how to get your client to agree to what you're proposing. But at the same time, you've got to know when there's nothing more to be gained from pursuing a conversation. That's the point at which it's probably best to push your chair away from the table, stand up, and count your winnings.

I had some painful experiences with this kind of situation, none more so than a couple of years ago when negotiating with a new client. We'd talked about just about everything that was on my agenda, and it was becoming painfully obvious to me that we weren't going to come to an agreement. It wasn't a question of being apart on a few issues; it was more that we weren't even in the same country and speaking a common language. At a certain point in the discussion I pushed the papers in front of me around and said, "Look, I don't think we're going to get an agreement here, so why don't we step back from things and reconvene in a couple of weeks."

I was trying to cool things off and put some distance between us so we could, I hoped, re-approach things in a more rational state of mind. One of the problems with any negotiation over a sale is that things can get heated, and before you know it you're saying things that were best left unsaid. The philosophy of positive selling rests in large measure on finding areas of agreement, but sometimes there's just not that much you can agree on.

In this instance, though, the client didn't want to handle things that way. After four or five hours in a continuous state of conflict, he glared at me and said, "No, let's just finish this up here and now."

For me, that was it. It was as clear as it could be that there was no reasonable way he and I could work together. Even if we'd ironed out the main points of disagreement—and there was no indication that we could—I didn't believe we could ever forge a long-term agreement that would lead to a profitable relationship.

I was more than ready for a fight with him. I was aching for it.

However, there are ways to walk away from a sale, and there are ways to run. I chose to walk. I said, very calmly (well, calm for me, anyway), "Look, it's clear that this isn't going to work. We just disagree on too many things. I'd like to think I can do something useful for you, but you clearly don't think so. Let's stop this discussion and both move on to something else."

Because I've trained myself to never, every shut doors, I then said, "I hope that in the next few months or years we can come back to the table and pick up this conversation. I assure you that I'll be just as willing to work with your company as I am at this moment."

Of course, in a sales fairy tale he'd sit down at the table and say something along the lines of, "Well, Steve, I certainly appreciate your honesty, and I think we need to start this discussion again."

In fact, what he said was halfway between a grunt and a growl— with a couple of swear words tossed in between. I kept my thoughts to myself and walked out the door. Six months later, he was ousted from his position with the company, and I wound up having a long, profitable relationship with his successor. I'd like to think it was karma. In fact, it was good, reasonable salesmanship on my part.

THE WALK AWAY POINT

Walking away from a sale is going to be one of the hardest things you do in your career. That's because it runs against everything you've ever been taught, everything that's part of your instinctual response as a salesperson. After all, I've told you in this book, and in others, that running into an objection just means you've encountered an opportunity. Nonetheless, you need to recognize that some sales can't be rescued, and you need to step back from them and wait for a better opportunity. The question is: How do you recognize one when it comes?

There are some clear signs that you should recognize:

1. **You're hitting the same points over and over again.**
    Rather than breaking new ground, you're simply rehashing the tired old issues over and over. Nothing is moving forward, and it's clear that you're covering the same ground.

2. **Neither of you is budging on the most important points.**
    Even though you may be making some progress in negotiating smaller issues, on the major questions that divide you, you're both sticking hard to your positions.

3. **The discussion is descending into personal issues.** The ancient Greeks and Romans, who were a very useful model as salespeople, spent a lot of time analyzing arguments and explaining how, precisely, they worked. One kind of argument they delineated was *ad hominem*, which means, roughly, "directed at the man." Ad hominem arguments are ones that depart from the issues and concentrate instead on the personalities of your opponents. If you find that you're getting to those sorts of conversations with your counterpart, you need to stop. And stop now. Such discussions won't go any place useful.

4. **Issues haven't matured.** It's entirely possible that the client hasn't quite gotten to the point where he is really ready to have a discussion with you. He may be in the middle of a transition in his company, and if that's the case, it may be

best for you to come back later. This is where your research will come in handy, since it will tell you what stage the transition is at and where it's likely to end up.

Whatever the case, you need to recognize that there are certain times when it's best not to proceed with the sale. From a positive standpoint, this means that a better opportunity awaits somewhere down the road. Positive selling is not always about forcing a sale here and now. It's about evaluating long-term prospects and making sure that you get the best possible deal, even if it takes a little longer to get there.

SAYING NO WHILE SAYING YES

If you decide to walk away, it's essential that you do so in a manner that tells the client you want to continue the discussion sometime later. This means leaving no hard feelings behind and at the same time arranging a specific time for follow up.

It also means that you don't have to assign blame for failure to conclude the sale. In fact, it's much better that you don't. You can simply say something along the lines of, "Well, Mr. Smith, it's pretty clear that we're a long way apart in these discussions. I think, rather than try to hammer out something here that neither of us will feel comfortable with, it might be better to let things sit for a couple of months. I suggest that we get back together at the end of September and see where we're at then. How would the 23rd work for you?"

As always, suggest a specific date for follow up. This makes it harder for the client to decline and commits both of you to a time in the future by which you'll have been able to work out at least some of your differences.

Once you get back to your office, be sure to draft a follow up memo to Mr. Smith. Cover what you agreed on first, followed by what you couldn't reach a conclusion on. Don't dwell on the disagreements; this is simply to make sure you're both on the same page. After you've covered that, summarize the main points of disagreement, remembering to present the client's point of view as fairly as possible. Then indicate any of the suggestions either of you made to resolve the points of disagreement.

Finish by re-stating at which point you've agreed to meet to resolve the issues that still lie between you. Ask for a confirmation of the date; if nothing else, this will serve to keep the correspondence going between you.

During the interim between when you've finished your last conversation and when you've scheduled the follow up meeting, find an excuse to stay in contact with the client. Send him articles you think he'd be interested in. Ask for his opinion about news items concerning the industry. Take several opportunities—without being obnoxious—to remind him of your upcoming meeting and the importance that you attach to resolving the disagreements that lie between you.

It's entirely possible that some of the big issues that you weren't able to resolve in your last meeting will have dissolved by the time you convene for a second conversation. Real life has a way of intervening and fixing things. But if this doesn't happen, be sure that when you're ready to meet again you've gone over all the outstanding issues and proposed solutions to them. Don't get involved in more ad hominem arguments; they're never productive, and you won't win them. Concentrate instead on finding win-win solutions to problems. With luck, you'll find that the client has been through a similar process, since it's very much in his interest to find a solution to these problems as well.

So when you walk away from a sale, remember, you're not really walking away permanently. You're just taking a necessary break.

WHEN THE CLIENT WALKS AWAY

29

John could put his finger on the exact moment when the sale went bad.

He'd been talking for about half an hour, running through the main points of his presentation smoothly and skillfully, asking the right questions, and keying off the answers. The responses hadn't been effusive, but he was feeling good about the tone of the meeting, ready to move toward closing.

Then the client leaned forward a bit, hands folded in front of him.

"John," he said, "I don't want to waste your time."

The temperature in the conference room dropped fifteen degrees. A minute before John had been mentally calculating his commission. Now he felt as if someone had pulled his chair away from under him.

"I don't quite understand," he heard himself saying.

The executive smiled. "I appreciate all the things you've told us," he said, "and I have to say that you make a very convincing presentation. But the fact of the matter is that we're just not ready to buy at this point, and I don't see why we should keep talking as if we're going to get to a deal when I know we're not."

John could feel his face flushing. He'd spent *hours* on this damn presentation. It had taken him an hour and forty minutes to get there, driving through bumper-to-bumper traffic in sweltering heat with his air conditioning kicking in and out. And now the guy was saying there wasn't even any point to his having come at all.

He tried to keep his voice steady. "When you say you're not ready to buy, don't you think that's a decision you should make only after you and I review all the facts and figures?"

The executive shook his head. "Nope. We're just not ready. I don't think we'll be ready to review this again for a couple of months either." He stood up and stuck out a hand. "I certainly appreciate you coming in . . ."

John stood up and slammed his briefcase on the table. Hands trembling, he crammed his papers into it. "You wasted my time," he snarled. "If you think I'm going to come back here and waste another couple of hours on the off chance that you might—*might*—be ready to buy in a few months, you're crazy."

The executive glared at him. "Well, there's certainly no point now!" he almost shouted. "We're done here!" And he stalked out. John followed a minute later, slamming the door behind him for good measure.

THE FAILED SALES CALL

It's happened to me more than I care to admit, and I can absolutely guarantee that in the course of your career it's going to happen to you: Someone is going to push too many of your buttons, and you're going to stand up and walk out of a presentation. The fact of the matter is, we're human beings, and just like anyone else we have tension, anger, frustration, often bubbling away below the surface, ready to break through.

And sometimes, either we do something or the client does something and the whole deal goes out the window. I can't tell you how to prevent this from ever happening in your career. I can tell you how to minimize it, though, and how to repair the damage afterward.

Start from the fact that whatever happens on a sales call, it's rarely personal. In a few instances it is—it's possible that you or your predecessor have done something to rub the client the wrong way. But usually you'll hear about that in advance and have a chance to fix it.

A friend of mine, some time back, walked into a sales presentation to find the entire department sitting in a row behind the table, glaring at him. He asked what was wrong, and they told him that he'd collectively insulted them in an e-mail, and they were there to demand satisfaction.

It was, he told me, one of the most disconcerting moments of his career. He mouthed something while frantically scrolling back in his mind through the e-mails he'd sent to folks from this company. Then the VP in charge of the division spoke up. "In your last note," he said, "you told us our launch date was a month early. Do you understand how insulting that is? You're saying we don't even understand our own industry!"

My friend had thought his comment was pretty innocuous when he made it—he was just trying to suggest that moving the date back would probably result in greater sales. But he'd obviously touched a nerve, and the VP had spread the word through the entire department. It seemed clear to my friend (and still does) that the executive was using this manufactured blow-up as an excuse to reinforce his authority within the company. This illustrates a point worth bearing in mind when a deal goes south: You don't necessarily know all the various undercurrents at play within a company. Sometimes the stated reason for a client raising objections or even walking away isn't the real reason, so don't automatically interpret it personally.

In this case, my friend apologized and explained that there had been a misunderstanding and that in no way was he trying to tell the company its business. By doing so, he was able to get the sales call back on track. Of course, he *could* have reacted personally and yelled and banged on the table. But that would have accomplished nothing. It's far better in these situations to put your ego in your back pocket and focus on your real goals.

DON'T CLOSE THE DOOR

The worst thing about reacting emotionally when a client tells you she doesn't want to buy is that you risk shutting down any possibility of a future relationship. Harking back to the example of John with which I started this chapter, do you think that there's any possibility that the company executive is ever going to want to do business with John again? What's far more likely is that the moment John has exited the building, the exec will be on the phone to John's boss, complaining about his unprofessional behavior. Whatever momentary satisfaction John obtained from slamming the door is going to be lost when he gets back to his office and starts trying to explain the loss of the sale to his superiors.

What would have been far more sensible would have been for John to have kept his emotions in check and said something along the lines of this: "Well, I understand your decision, but I don't want to lose touch in the intervening time. How about if we set up a weekly phone call just to touch base. Would Wednesdays at 10 AM work for you?" He had a clear opening for that, because the executive didn't say his company would *never* buy—just that they weren't going to buy that day.

When a client is walking away from a deal, your number one priority is to continue the sales relationship. That's the only hope you have of salvaging something from the hard work you've put into this project. Ask for a follow up meeting, send e-mails, and make phone calls—do anything you have to in order to remain in touch with the client.

It's particularly important, when you get back to the office after a failed sales call, to do two things:

1. **Send a note to your boss, detailing exactly what happened and why.** The note should explain not only that you failed to close the deal, but what your plans are for follow up. You want to project a positive attitude toward keeping this client and eventually making a sale.

2. **Send an e-mail to the client, thanking her for her time and summarizing your conversation.** This should be instinctual after any sales call, but it's especially essential after one that failed. Again, the purpose is to keep the sales relationship and set the stage for future deals.

If, by some chance, you've been abrupt or angry in the way you ended the sales call, don't wait for the client to get back to you. Call her right away and apologize. You can explain that you were caught by the suddenness of her announcement and that you want to maintain a good relationship with her company. It's important to smooth over any ruffled feathers.

That applies as well if the client's the one who stomped out of the meeting. I know it's harder to do when you're talking to someone who's being completely unreasonable. It's worth making the effort, though. Remember what I said about what might be currently under the surface. Sometimes the client just needs a chance to get out of the room and calm down a bit before returning to rationality.

WHEN IS A SALE NOT A SALE?

As a last point, you need to be able to recognize when a client is negotiating and when he's really walking away from a sale. The two can look remarkably similar sometimes. If you go back to the example at the beginning of this chapter, it's possible that, had John not started to boil over immediately, he might have wondered if the executive was simply trying to take an aggressive negotiating posture, one aimed at throwing John off his step. (John, in fact, never determined this and so never knew if he'd completely blown a sale that with a bit more effort he might have made.)

When a client announces he's not going to buy and that you're not going to sell, do what you should always do: Ask questions.

Find out why. Find out if this objection can be overcome. Find out if you're talking to the right person—someone authorized to close the sale. Above all, find out if the client really wants to stop the sales call or if he's just waiting for you to come back with another proposal. You can usually find out the answer to this last question simply by proposing to close the deal: "I understand that you don't feel we can conclude a sale right now, but I'd like to suggest that there are some terms on which maybe we can do business."

In many cases, you'll find that the client backs down and the meeting goes on. In other instances, though, it will become clear that the client just isn't going to buy, in which case, you need to respect his decision. Getting angry or insulting him will accomplish nothing and will ensure that you'll lose his account forever.

Don't argue. Make an appointment for a follow up meeting or phone call, pack up your things, and leave.

And don't slam the door.

BUILDING FOR THE LONG TERM

30

I was sitting in the back of the room, a notepad on my knee. Around me, eager executives were perched on the edge of their chairs, leaning forward as the young man strode up to the podium. It was a gathering of businessmen to talk about careers and career prospects. The guy now straightening notes preparatory to tossing out the first sentence of his talk was something of a *wunderkind*, so everyone was interested in what he'd have to say.

He started by explaining that five years previously, after much struggle, he'd landed his dream job. He was working in the front office of a sports team, doing what he loved, rubbing shoulders with the players on a day-to-day basis. He traveled with the team, watched all the games, and sat in meetings with the owners and executives who made decisions about trades and strategy. He'd followed sports since he was a kid—and this particular sport was his favorite.

No question: He *loved* his job.

"But then," he said, "I realized that I wasn't going to go any higher in the organization. I wasn't making the kind of money I needed to make. So I took a hard look at other industries. And now I'm in this industry, bringing my experience to it and ready to contribute what I learned from organized sports."

The whole room broke into applause. Well, except for me. I sat there with my mouth open. As soon as the meeting ended and I got back to my hotel room, I called members of my family. I was practically shouting.

"You won't believe this guy! He had his dream job! *His dream job!* And he gave it up to make more money. What happened to passion? What happened to what he loved? *His dream job!*"

The whole thing hit a nerve for me because it seemed so tragic. Of the millions and millions of us who get up every Monday morning and brace ourselves at the thought of another work-week, how many can say to themselves, "I'm going to work at a place I've dreamed of since I was a little kid"? How many of us can fulfill our passion through our work? The answer is, not many. Most of us try to do our jobs well and be professional, but we're motivated primarily by the thought of a paycheck at the end of every month. Here was a guy experiencing this sort of amazing personal joy as a result of his job, and he'd given it up to go into an industry for which he had no particular attachment, and that was going to give him no significant measure of satisfaction except for more money.

How tragic is that?

SALES AS A CAREER

I've been fortunate enough over the years to enjoy what I do. I like helping to shape salespeople's careers and improve them. I like dealing with the range of problems and personalities that comes with the territory of sales. And I have to admit that there's a part of my ego that's gratified by the accolades that have come my way. It's possible, I suppose, that I could have made more money doing something else, but it wouldn't have given me the same degree of personal satisfaction that I've derived from my career.

In this book I've stressed over and over again the virtues of being positive and finding an affirmative way to overcome the difficulties of an average (and occasionally not so average) sales call. It seems to me that the first step in this positive attitude is this: You have to like what you do.

In a previous chapter, I mentioned the difference between those who see sales as a job and those who see it as a career. That's the starting point for positive salesmanship: the belief that you're in this for the long haul. To the career salesperson, sales is something she likes doing. It isn't that she has no other interests in life—in fact, I'd argue that being a well-rounded person makes you a better salesperson—but sales makes her feel good about herself and stimulates her intellectually. She enjoys meeting and talking to people. She likes to find out what makes them tick and what they want. She finds satisfaction in solving problems and in confronting and overcoming difficulties. She's firm and disciplined, but she knows the value of compromise. She knows how to elicit information without seeming to intrude.

At the same time, she's a bit of a psychologist. She wants to understand why people make the decisions they do and how they get themselves through the day. She's persuasive, of course—you can't be a salesperson without the ability to argue for your opinion. But she knows that there's a bigger picture and that it's part of her job to discover it.

I've just painted a picture of what I believe to be a Positive Salesperson. There's nothing of the Pollyanna in her. I find it really annoying to be around people who are relentlessly cheerful and upbeat. But at the same time, I don't want to hang around someone who's constantly gloomy and never sees any good in any situation. The positive salesperson has a nice balance between these two extremes.

WHAT DO YOU *LIKE* TO DO?

Most of us find parts of our job interesting and engaging. But there are long stretches of boredom or, eventually, burnout. I've seen a lot of salespeople—men and women who've been in the profession ten, twenty, or thirty years—who just don't care any more. Sometimes they make a big sale, but mostly they're not selling; they're taking orders. They make the rounds of the same clients, over and over again, pitch the same line they've always used, and get a modest order that's usually a bit smaller than the last time. People like that will eventually put themselves out of a job. They become a drain on everyone and everything around them, and an organization that is dominated by them won't last. Any successful company has to be driven by passion.

Look at Apple. A lot of people said bad things about Steve Jobs over the years, and I have no doubt that he was a difficult man to work for. But I've never heard anyone deny his passion for the company he created and the products it made. That's why so many Mac fans are practically religious in their adoration of their iPads, iPods, iPhones, and iMacs.

Consider Warren Buffett. The guy's a multi-billionaire, with more money than anyone else on the planet. But he still goes to work every morning. Why? He doesn't need to. He could retire today and spend the rest of his life playing bridge—something Buffett likes to do, apparently. But he still goes to work, because he likes it. He feels strongly about it. When he was young, he read a book on investing by Benjamin Graham, and it influenced him. He wanted to know how money worked, and how money could beget money. He found it fascinating, and that fascination has lasted him the rest of his life.

It would be nice if we could all become billionaires, but even if that doesn't happen, I think we can find work that motivates us. And if we haven't found it yet, we should keep looking.

This is what I mean by being positive. It's not a matter of ignoring problems or trying to pretend the sky is blue when it's gray and rainy. It's caring enough to do something about it. If you care about what you're selling, who you're selling it to, and the whole process of sales, you'll see specific benefits. Your commissions will tend to be higher, you'll suffer less from feelings of burnout, and you'll find that your life becomes happier and more interesting.

LOOKING BEYOND THE MOMENT

Throughout this book, I've stressed the importance of maintaining a long-term sales relationship with your clients. That's not something you can do if you're just taking orders and going through the motions. Competition is fierce, and if you don't care about what you're doing, your clients and prospects are going to find someone who does. But building and maintaining that relationship takes work.

1. **Every week, call or e-mail your most important clients.** Chat with them about how they're feeling, how your product or service is working for them, and what they think about the latest developments in their industry and the world in general. Sometimes the subject of the talk is less important than just the communication itself.

2. **Stay on the lookout for interesting articles, books, or online materials that you can send to your contacts.**

3. **Use social media to widen your circle of contacts.** LinkedIn is a particularly helpful network that's used by business professionals. Other people are increasingly making use of social networking platforms such as Twitter and Facebook to enlarge their business circles.

4. **Don't assume, when calling on a long-established client, that his needs and concerns are going to be exactly the same as they've always been.** We're living through one of the greatest economic realignments in several generations, and things are changing very fast. It's quite possible that since you last spoke, your client has encountered a crisis that he's never faced before, and he'll want your help in solving it.

5. **When you walk into a sales call, stop a moment and remind yourself of why you're doing this.** It's more than a paycheck. It's a conviction that you're doing something worthwhile, something that's contributing to the well-being of others. You're helping a company stay in business, employing workers and keeping a section of the American economy going, however small it may be. You're providing something that others want and need.

That should be the mantra of every salesperson. At the end of the day, when you're facing another executive, another buyer, another group of people who are looking at you and thinking, "Yeah? What've *you* got to say to us?" all you've got is your integrity, your energy, and your Attitude.

And that's enough to make the sale.

INDEX